The Sevenfold Shaman

The Sevenfold Shaman

§

S.R. Lampman

The cover image is a twenty-eight-thousand- year-old cave painting from southwestern France called the Shaman of Trois Frères. The antlers have seven points, three lower and four higher. Antlers are a symbol of regeneration because they yield a velvet skin that sheds each spring until maturity. The seven points designates a complete transformation to sevenfold, the whole and completed shaman. It is a prehistoric image reminiscent of Shiva, lord of the dance.

ISBN-13: 9780692700099
ISBN-10: 0692700099
Library of Congress Control Number: 2016907211
S. R. Lampman, Bellingham, WA

For Sean Michael and the fortunate generation he represents.*

---

* This is a reference to the Judas Gospel, Scenes 1–2

Contents

Introduction

§

"Again, and maybe for the last time on this
earth, I recall the great vision that you sent me.
It may be that some little root of the sacred
tree still lives. Nourish it then, that it may
leaf and bloom and fill with singing birds".*

THE AIM OF THIS LITTLE book** is to shed light on the mystic's
experience, giving special attention to the visionary phenomena at the beginning—which tends to start new religions—and
the different levels of illumination possible for the founders
(i.e., the rank and order of schizotypal leaders and the religions
they spawn).

Humans can gain extensive knowledge on a subject and
then lose it again for hundreds if not thousands of years, until
another person does the necessary work to recover it. Consider,
for example, Aristarchus of Samos who in 300BCE outlined
knowledge of our sun-centered planetary system. After his
death, that knowledge was lost for nearly eighteen hundred
years—until the time of Copernicus.

---

* (Black Elk Speaks, John G Neihardt, William Morrow & Company, 1932, 233)
** This is a reference to the "Little Book" cited in chapter ten of Revelations.

Likewise knowledge concerning the "visions" that initiated major holy men into their careers—a phenomenon recorded universally in religious texts—has been lost for centuries, if not millennia. Thousands of years ago, the Jewish elders told their prophets to put knowledge away until the end time.

That time they spoke of has arrived; fulfillment of prophecy is at hand.

"There is nothing hidden that will not be
disclosed, and nothing concealed that will not
be known or brought out into the open".

(LUKE 8:17)

CHAPTER 1

§

VISIONS, EGO-DEATH AND REBIRTH

RELIGIONS WOULD NOT EXIST, WERE it not for the unusual, stress-induced visionary experiences of the founders. Modern anthropologists, evolutionary psychiatrists and others call this phenomena (that spawns new religions), primary mazeway resynthesis (PMR). This is a fancy name for a vision that causes a psychological death and spiritual rebirth. Noted anthropologist Anthony F. Wallace, PhD, coined the term in the 1950s:

> "The re-synthesis is most dramatically exemplified in the career of the prophet, who formulates a new religious code during a hallucinatory trance. Typically, such persons, after suffering increasing depreciation of self-esteem as the result of their inadequacy to achieve the culturally ideal standards, reach a point of either physical or drug induced exhaustion, during which a resynthesis of values and beliefs occurs. The resynthesis is, like other innovations, a recombination of preexisting configurations. The uniqueness of this particular process is the suddenness of conviction, the trance like state of the subject, and the emotionally central nature of the subject matter".*

---

* (Anthony F. Wallace "Mazeway Resynthesis: A Biocultural Theory of Religious Inspiration", Transactions of the New York Academy of Sciences, 1956, 626-638)

"Mazeway" essentially means worldview, including your socialization, religious beliefs, indoctrination, education, self-image, etc. PMR visions can fundamentally change a person's view, by providing them with—what appears at first to be—a glimpse into the inner workings of the spirit realm.

Contrary to popular belief, the visions of the prophets of old still happen today, exactly as they have since the dawn of humanity. Nonetheless, most religious folk adhere to a viewpoint called cessationism.

Religious cessationists believe the visions of men like Moses, the Buddha, Saint Paul, Muhammad, etc., stopped happening long ago. It's true that the ability to *recognize* them has been lost for a long time. But believing that on the two-hundred-thousand-year timeline of our species, ecstatic visions happened only around the time of the Roman Empire is to accept the "highly-unlikely".

Wallace used some recent examples to illustrate his theory of mazeway resynthesis, hysterical conversion and revitalization movements. For instance, Hung Hsiu-ch'üan had a visionary experience that inspired the Taiping Rebellion of southern China in 1851. American missionaries converted Hsiu-ch'üan to Christianity; soon after he experienced a powerful vision, a visitation.

From an old man he interpreted as "God the Father". In the same way the famous Catholic saint Joan of Arc had a vision that inspired her to throw the English out of France during the Hundred Years War, Hsiu-ch'üan had a vision that convinced him it was his destiny to restore the "true faith" to China. And this could only be done by overthrowing the Manchu Imperial Dynasty, which he and his followers nearly toppled.

Similarly, the "Ghost Dance" came from a man named Wovoka of the Paiute tribe, son of Tavibo and also a medicine man. Wovoka—aka Jack Wilson—was born on a reservation in

Mason Valley Nevada, in 1856. At the age of thirty-three, he experienced a dramatic PMR. During the vision, Wovoka "Saw God and all the people who had died a long time ago. God told me to come back and tell my people that they must be good and love one another and not fight or steal or lie". (Wovoka, 1889)

Note the Five Commandments.

Mottos like "people never change" are incorrect. A tiger cannot change its stripes, but human personalities can and do change. Usually sudden personality change is a bad thing (e.g., drug use, the onset of schizophrenia, brain damage, etc.), but it's a good thing when it's the product of a mystical experience. Spiritual development is usually a gradual process; however, sometimes enormous growth happens literally overnight. As a rule, to be eligible for a spiritual rebirth, one must first be depressed, afflicted, stressed to the point of exhaustion, and/or completely aimless in life. The visionary initiation resurrects the person from a death-like state of existence by revealing a true calling as a holy man or woman. Figuratively, the person's old sackcloth is removed, and he or she is clothed in gladness, set on high.

> "Nearly all are men, though history records some outstanding female examples, such as Joan of Arc. Of those for whom personal details exist, most would readily satisfy the DSM-4 criteria for borderline, schizotypal, or paranoid personality disorder. The most striking thing about them is their shamanic quality. The Tungus noun Saman means, "One who is excited, moved, raised". As a verb it means, "To know in an ecstatic manner". Ethnological studies of shamans in Siberia, Africa, and North America reveal them to be close to the borderline but not over it; they are schizotypal, not schizophrenic". (Anthony Stevens and John Price, *Evolutionary Psychiatry*,

A New Beginning simultaneously published in the USA
and Canada by Taylor and Francis Inc., 2000, 148)

Schizotypal personalities have strange beliefs. The weird ideas
can come from dreams, visions, or any other means. If they're
charismatic, articulate, and have leadership qualities, they may
influence others to have confidence in in their vision.

SECONDARY MAZEWAY RESYNTHESIS

Primary visions can have a remarkable secondary effect. When
a charismatic, schizotypal prophet gives people an account of
their vision, and others believe it wholeheartedly—evidenced
by a change of core belief and personality—the beginner mystic has unwittingly facilitated "secondary mazeway resynthesis", a type of religious conversion. Our ancestors called this
"anointing by God" and "baptism by fire".

Wise elders were once able to identify—if not rank—the
visions according to their degree of complexity. In fact, modern psychiatrists also make a distinction between genuine spiritual experiences and mental illness. The American Psychiatric
Association (APA), made a revision to the DSM3 (diagnostic
manual for mental illness, third edition), in 1993, to account for
these rare and unusually therapeutic experiences.

Over the last hundred years, psychiatrists acknowledged the
phenomena, with names like positive disintegration, visionary
states, and spiritual emergence. A new diagnostic category was
drawn out, submitted to the American Psychiatric Association
in 1991, and entered into the DSM4 in 1994, listed as code
V.62.89 A Religious or Spiritual Crisis.

The first problem for the up-and-coming prophet is this:
In order to benefit from the experience, that is, in order
to gain the therapeutic effects of the vision—and they are

considerable—the initiate must wholeheartedly believe what they experienced during the vision was real, not just a figment of their imagination. But paradoxically, in order to progress to higher levels of spiritual understanding, the newly transformed must question what has happened to them, and then, perhaps oddly, as if looking a gift horse from God in the mouth, the visionary phenomena (e.g., angels, demons, ghosts, aliens, past lives, etc.) must be reexamined and understood as subjective.

"There, likewise, I beheld Excalibur.
Before him at his crowning borne,
"The sword, that rose from out
the bosom of the lake,
"And Arthur row'd across and took it-rich
with jewels, elfin Urim, on the hilt.
"Bewildering heart and eye—the blade so bright
that men are blinded by it—on one side, graven
in the oldest tongue in the world, 'Take me,'
"But turn the blade and ye shall see, and written
in the speech ye speak yourself, 'Cast me away'"!

(TENNYSON, *IDYLLS OF THE KING*).

CHAPTER 2

§

THE FISHERMAN'S RING

"What we are doing, I have discovered from
years of theoretical research and clinical
observation, is looking for someone who has

the predominant character traits of the people
who raised us. Our old brain, trapped in the
eternal now and having only a dim awareness
of the outside world, is trying to recreate the
environment of childhood. And the reason the
old brain is trying to resurrect the past is not
a matter of habit or blind compulsion but of a
compelling need to heal old childhood wounds".

(HARVILLE HENDRIX, *GETTING
THE LOVE YOU WANT*, SIMON AND
SCHUSTER, NEW YORK, 2005, 14)

BY THE TIME I MET Madeline, I'd been fishing in the Bering
Sea for almost fourteen years. For those of you unfamiliar with
the operation, we stack a couple of hundred 7 x 7-foot pots on
the deck. After tying each pot down with a small piece of line
called a "pot tie", we then chain the whole stack down using the
same kind of chain and binders that trucker's use.

After chaining down the stack, we load up on food, fuel and
bait—then head to the fishing grounds. When we get within a
few hours of where the captain wants to set the pots, the greenhorn starts getting the bait jars ready, so when we get there,
we can start setting "strings" of twenty to thirty pots right
away. My job as stack-man was to climb to the top of the stack,
unchain the pots, and then untie each pot individually, before
hooking them up to the crane.

One night while working the stack in rough weather, about
halfway through setting the two-hundred-pot deck load (and
after screaming at countless greenhorns to leave one pot tie
attached), I accidentally untied all four pot ties. Then as I
climbed on top of the pot—to hook the crane-strap through
the crossbars—the boat rolled hard to starboard, and the pot I
was standing on started sliding overboard with me on top!

I started to run in place as the pot moved like a treadmill beneath my feet! Managing to put my right foot on the outside bar, with all my leg strength, I jumped toward the boat, barely making it back to the stack! Beneath me, the pot splashed into the black water with the line and buoys still trapped inside.

Just then, the captain put the boat in neutral, setting us adrift. The wheelhouse door swung open and he stepped out and down the ladder. I thought he was angry about my suit-casing the pot, but he didn't even see it; no one did (suitcasing means setting the pot with the door shut, and with the line and buoys needed to retrieve it, trapped inside).

He was upset that he lost his wedding ring. A few months earlier, he got married in Korea to a Korean wife, and as part of the marriage ceremony her family had the ring hand-made. The ring was meant to symbolize the bride. It was a good fisherman's ring, because it didn't have any gemstones that could be snagged by a hook. Fishermen lose fingers that way.

The captain ordered us to look for the ring. I climbed down the engine room ladder into the bowels of the boat. After a quick glance, I sat down at the bottom of the stairs, and slept—as if a fog rolled over me.

Next thing I knew, the captain was calling me from on top of the stairs, "Wake up Lampman! We're on the gear".

Startled awake I mumbled back, "Here I am"!

We searched all over the boat but never found the ring. When the 1998, Opelio season was over, our crew flew home and a relief skipper drove the boat back down to Seattle. A month after getting home, I ran into Madeline at a party in north Seattle. When we first met, she had curly blonde hair, but now her hair was straight and red like my mom's used to be. She was the most attractive young woman there.

I grabbed the barstool directly across the bar from her, sat down and said, "Hi Madeline, remember me?"

Happily she did remember me. "Hey Scott, and didn't we party together at that dead guy's house?"

MADELINE

Her smile was just as I remembered, with one slightly crooked tooth. In a not-so-subtle attempt to determine her status, I asked how it had gone with her fiancé. I was inwardly pleased to hear they had broken-up some months ago, and then instantly deflated when she mentioned someone else she'd begun seeing recently. I looked down and then noticed her fidgeting with a gold ring—too big to fit on her fingers. I asked where it came from and she replied, "The guy I've been dating found it on a boat at the shipyard he works at".

I knew right away that it was my captain's and blurted out, "That's my captain's ring"! Madeline laughed skeptically thinking I was teasing her. But then I looked her straight in the eyes and said, "It's the truth. He stopped the whole operation while we searched the boat for it". Our captain didn't like to wait for us to arc-weld when a pot needed fixing. So whenever something broke on deck and needed arc welding, he would run down from the wheelhouse and weld it for us. After welding something on deck, the captain must have thrown the welding gloves onto the pile by the dryer, with the ring stuck inside. Nobody thought to look in the gloves for it.

I was doing my best to convince Madeline her boyfriend was a shmuck for not trying to return the ring. After a few drinks I suggested, together we should return it to my captain. Somehow, I ended up with Madeline and the ring that evening. The following day we called my captain. And at the appointed time, the fisherman's ring was returned.

Madeline and I started dating exclusively. After a year, she was pregnant. Strangely, my son's due date—printed on the ultrasound picture—was September 19, 1999, my thirty-second birthday. I rented us a small, three-bedroom house a few blocks up from the ferry terminal in Mukilteo, Washington. We were prepared as far as food, clothing and shelter—but not at all prepared emotionally. Nevertheless, my son was born at Steven's Memorial Hospital, on the autumn equinox morning on September, 22, 1999. I'd seen some amazing things in my life (e.g., a rogue wave, whales breaching to protect their young, phosphorous glowing like a green Milky Way on the surface of the ocean, the aurora borealis, etc.), but my son's crowning was the most amazing thing I'd ever seen.

After the umbilical cord was cut, the nurse handed Sean to me. His face was smooth and beautiful. Bewildered, I turned to the nurse and said softly, "I thought new babies were supposed to come out looking all prune-faced and ugly?"

She smiled and whispered, "They don't come out looking like this very often".

After Madeline fell asleep, I sat down in a chair by the window with Sean Michael sleeping in my arms. The sun was nearly gone, and in the silence, it grew duskier until I could see my own reflection in the window. As it got darker, I noticed there was a small fire burning at the bottom of the hill, as if someone had set a dumpster on fire. It was far enough away as to not pose a threat to us, but clearly visible from the window. As the minutes ticked by and the flames grew larger, I wondered, where the fire trucks were. With Sean snoozing in my arms, I walked out to the nurses' station to tell them about the fire. We all hurried over to the window. The smell of smoke had entered the building, and off in the distance we heard the sound of fire-truck sirens responding to the fire.

By the time they got their hoses hooked up, it was burning out of control, shooting out of every open door; even setting the adjacent bushes on fire. I went back to our maternity room and tried waking Madeline up, so she could see the amazing fire. I shook her foot and said, "Madeline, wake up, there's a building on fire at the bottom of the hill".

She opened one eye and said, "Don't wake me up, unless the building I'm in is on fire"! Then she rolled over and fell back to sleep. Too softly to be heard, I sat back down in the chair—still holding my son.

I spent the night gawking at the building fire and beholding the face of my newborn son. It turned out the fire started due to an electrical problem in the kitchen of the China Passage Restaurant. As the sun came up over the Cascade Mountains in the east, I could see the place where the China Passage once stood; the terrain was as flat as a roof.

Madeline and I never argued before. But as autumn turned to winter, and each day got shorter and darker, it seemed that I was likewise descending into the pit of depression. On the last day of November 1999, Madeline was berating me for getting her fast food order wrong. She was three inches from my face, screaming at the top of her lungs. And when she moved in closer to my face, and her spit hit my face, I pecked her in the forehead with the brim of my ball cap—like a drill sergeant does to new recruits. She wasn't hurt, but nevertheless immediately ran for the phone to call the police.

When she dialed 9-1-1, I panicked and ripped the phone off the wall. But the call went through. The police station was just a few blocks away; they'd be responding immediately. With this realization, I started running around the house, looking for my shoes, so I could run away, but they were nowhere to be found.

I'd never hit a girl in my life (not even the older sister I grew up with as kids). But I snapped, and—like a wild animal—I charged her from across the living room. She ran into Sean's nursery and picked him up from his crib, and held him up in front of her, using him as a shield. I grabbed her arm and Sean dropped to the floor with a thud, as police officers kicked the front door in. Luckily the floor was well carpeted.

I released Madeline and ran into the living room, where an officer was standing on my door like a surfer riding a surfboard. His 9mm pistol was drawn and pointed at my chest as he yelled, "Get on the floor"! He promptly arrested me; after spending the night in jail, I was released the next morning. Madeline was surprised to see me. I apologized and promised never to hurt her again. Then I went over to Sean's rocker, where he was swinging back and forth, happily playing with a baby toy.

As I approached from across the room, he looked up, but instead of the usual happy face, his eyes grew wide with terror. As I reached down to pick him up, he put his tiny shaking hands up in front of his face, as if to protect himself—from me attacking him. I turned and snapped at Madeline for using him as a shield. From his perspective, it must have seemed like I was charging at him.

After holding Sean for a minute, he calmed down, and I thought, it's a good thing he's too young to remember any of this. A few days later, on Christmas Eve, Madeline finally left with Sean, exactly as my mother did, thirty-two years earlier, a few days before Christmas, when I was three months old. Too ashamed to see my family, I spent that Christmas morning (and day) alone.

Christmas night I went to my friend Erin's place. Once there, I started complaining about a long list of things that were bothering me. I went on and on about how my father was a heroin addict who killed himself, how my stepdad was an abusive, alcoholic that beat me daily as my mother looked the other way, and how my girlfriend was decapitated by a drunk driver and my closest family friend died of a heroin overdose, etc. Madeline leaving with Sean on Christmas Eve was similarly traumatic.

Erin began to cry when I shook my head and whispered, "I have this weird feeling my death is right around the corner". On my way home the motor in my truck seized up, so that it was completely broken down. Over the next few days, the usual feelings of loss, self-loathing, and self-pity—that I'd felt since my youth—morphed into real suicidal depression. I couldn't understand why I had to endure so much suffering? What could I have possibly done to deserve all this loss and misery? Perhaps I'd done something terrible in a past life, and I was paying for it now. I didn't know. It felt like I was being buried under a mountain of emotional pain that kept growing and growing. With no conceivable way for the mountain to ever stop growing, I decided to spare myself the future misery and commit suicide.

I started giving my belongings away and planning my departure. Everything seemed to be happening according to a grand plan; soon my suffering would be over. As the millennia approached, I wished for an apocalypse—like the Y2K glitch—but the turn of the millennium was uneventful, or so it seemed.

On the morning of January 4, 2000, my friend Arthur showed up to collect the money I owed him for a quarter pound of pot. But I'd been on a binge, and spent most of his cash. We both should've been on our way to Alaska on crab boats, at that time of year. But for the first time ever, the Alaska Department of Fish and Game decided to postpone the Opelio crab season, due to low numbers in the test pots (also called prospect pots).

Arthur asked for the money I owed him. Acting as if it were no big deal I said, "Don't worry dude, I'll have your money in a couple days. I'm not going to screw you over".

Arthur replied sternly, "You told me you'd have the money today, and I need the money today, so you have already screwed me over"!

I looked down and sighed in defeat, as I had a million times before, trying to think of an excuse. But my mind was drawing a blank, because there wasn't one. So I said honestly, "Arthur, I'm really sorry, there's no excuse".

He paused, as if remembering something important, then looked me square in the eyes and said, "Scott, it's OK; I forgive you".

Oblivious to what he meant—I snapped back, "What the fuck do you mean, you forgive me?"

Arthur sighed and then assured me "Don't worry brother; I forgive you. It's only money. You can pay me back later, or if you want, you can help me with my back-yard pond project". Then he walked back to his truck and smiled as he drove off.

I had a concept of what the word meant, but had never actually been forgiven for anything before. I'd only ever thought to seek revenge when wronged. It seemed like a bit of weight was lifted off a very heavy load. It was enough for me to postpone killing myself for the time being.

The next morning he picked me up and we started the job. His wife Rachel had never seen Sean. So after getting home that night (January 5), I removed his baby pictures from the frames set on top of the entertainment center, and put them in my day planner.

EPIPHANY ON THE EPIPHANY

On the morning of the sixth, and after we arrived at his house, I showed the pictures to Arthur and his wife Rachel, and then we got to work. After digging a pit for the pond—and lamenting again all day—at about four o'clock the thunder clouds started rolling in, so Arthur gave me a ride home. On the way, we stopped at Home Depot to pick up some landscape materials. Arthur went inside while I used the payphone outside. After a few minutes he came out with a bunch of cement on a cart, which I helped him load into the truck. After loading the bags of cement, we headed towards my place.

A few miles down the road, I realized that I'd left my day planner back at the phone booth, with all my son's baby pictures in it. Arthur turned around, but by the time we got back, it was gone. After talking with the manager, it was clear the planner wasn't turned in there. Dumbfounded, I realized I'd just lost all my son's baby pictures. I didn't realize until then, they were my most valued possessions. The irony struck me, that the pictures were as worthless to whoever took the day planner as they were valuable to me. I imagined filthy hands, throwing them into the garbage. Then the feelings of impending doom came, a sickening feeling, as if I had just lost something my life depended on.

Arthur drove me home, dropping me off at my lifeless house, at about five o'clock on the evening of January 6, 2000. I sat down and turned on the tube, and then clicked the channel to MTV2, thinking some music videos might cheer me up. Looking in my son's empty room was way too disturbing, so I shut the door, and then sat back down on the couch to watch the videos. After a few minutes, a song by a band called Filter came on titled "Take a Picture".

Soon the chorus of the song was blaring, "Could you take my picture, because I won't remember?" The lyrics struck a chord within me, reminding me of an equally painful truth I never admitted. I didn't have any pictures of my father either. And with that thought, the chorus of the Filter song sounded again, "Does everybody agree that no one should be left alone?"

The thought of my father forsaking me—by committing suicide and leaving me fatherless—caused me to leap up from the couch enraged. Filled with the kind anger that men use to force back tears, I glanced down at my left palm, at a scar I got long-lining crab pots, when a Victorinox deck knife pierced my hand nearly all the way through. After clenching my left palm into a tight fist I cried out, "No pictures of my father"! Then I looked down at another deep scar—on the palm of my right hand (from a chainsaw accident)—and likewise clenched it into a tight fist and cried out, "No pictures of my son"! Then with both fists clenched as tightly as possible, with my fingernails digging into my skin, I raised my arms up to the sky and—along with the lyrics of the song—cried out, "Hey Dad, what do you think about your son now?"

Abruptly, my father's spirit appeared in front of me, on his knees with his arms around my waist, and his head in my bosom. An overwhelming sense of guilt, shame and regret—emanated from his tortured ghost; evidently because he had to witness the enduring pain he caused his family and friends by committing suicide. A chill ran down my spine as I mumbled to myself, "I must be losing it".

After turning off the TV, I quickly ran around the house turning on every light in the place. My first instinct was to leave, but there was a storm raging outside, and my truck motor was blown. I wanted to call someone, but I had no phone, because I'd ripped it off the wall during a fight with Madeline.

There was always someone around when I needed to talk, either on the phone or in person. Or there was somewhere to drive, something to watch on TV, etc. Even in the middle of the Bering Sea there were people to talk to. But for some reason, on this night, there was nobody, and nothing to ease my mind, from the fear I was losing it.

In an effort to get my mind off these unsettling thoughts, I started looking for a distraction; a pencil and notebook were all I could find. So, with paper and pencil in hand, I sat back down on the couch. Outside, the wind was howling, blowing sheets of rain and sleet against the windows. I began writing a poem about how my son might be feeling about his parents fighting and breaking up. But in order to do this, I had to put myself in his shoes and try to see the situation through his eyes.

And as I beheld our fighting through his innocent, three month old eyes, I was suddenly horrified. From his viewpoint, I was a frightening monster. The terror also came from seeing how far I'd strayed from my original innocence, how corrupted I'd become. My consciousness was like a corrupted hard drive, clogged with useless programs, and depressing pictures. When I saw what the world had made of me, I finally burst into tears, wailing loud like a baby.

Madeline and I were so busy fighting—both in our own little worlds—we never paused to considered how we might be affecting *his* little world.

I thought about what he might say if he could speak. I imagined him saying, "Please stop fighting, it's too scary"! "Please just love each other, as I love you".

With tears gushing down the side of my face, and dripping off my chin, I begin to write a poem that changed my life:

A child forsaken, true love mistaken
For just another false front.
Run away love taught young
Provides a spot for feelings to rot.
Hitting, screaming, throwing and bleeding,
Serenity fading, no faith or forgiveness, no healing.
New parent frustration, the foundation,
For another painful separation,
Controlling, conditional love runs away,
A carbon copy baby yesterday,
Just a baby today.
Death threats and stolen redemption,
Cause broken homes, loss, guilt and depression.
Taught to deny my father's suicide,

To suppress my pain deep inside my severed brain,
Ability inefficiency, I'm less than, lost potential,
Taught in infancy that life is hard,
That love, family, and everything dear,
Are short-term blessings that all disappear.

It took a couple hours to finish the first part of the poem. I would write something about how my parents failed me, how I failed my son, etc., then examine it closer, cry a bit, have some epiphany, then erase some and re-write it.

I used the eraser so much—it started to wear holes through the paper. Then, about halfway through the first stanza, I realized I wasn't writing about my son at all. I was writing about *my* parents' break-up, as well as the loss of my father.

By having compassion for my son, I was inadvertently re-experiencing *my* parents break-up—and the loss of my father—at the same age (three months old). It was this first loss—not the things I usually blamed—that was the original cause of my depression. The realization that I had just unwittingly traumatized my son in exactly the same way, made me cry even harder.

Weird coincidences were starting to make sense. But it wasn't chance. I realized my maternal grandmother also left my grandfather, exactly as my mom did. I wondered how many generations, this broken home cycle went back. It was evidently some kind of repeating cycle. It was as if I was pre-programmed to break up with Madeline, by following my parent's bad example. It struck me; I was taught how to break up a family, when I was so young, I could *only* learn by example! Feeling righteous indignation—perhaps for the first time—I said aloud, "I was taught too young how to break up my family"! The memory of my stepdad breaking my mom's nose—during a drunken fight—came to mind. Clearly, my fighting with Madeline was an echo of that abuse.

(Above, history repeats itself perfectly. On the left is a photo of Madeline and me taken before she left on Christmas Eve. On the right is a picture of my mother and father, Donna and Robert Lampman—with the same expressions on their faces— taken days before Christmas, just prior to their break-up.)

Getting F's and D's in school—due to undiagnosed ADD— led me to believe I was stupid and bad. I suddenly realized I wasn't bad, I was just raised badly! After crying for a while— though strangely not in self-pity—I finally calmed down, and started writing the next phase of the poem, which actually was about my son:

> Carbon copy baby boy in the light,
> I was taught young to do this right.
> To fight and scream and blame and be mean,
> To make it clear the front is false,
> And in our fake family there's no love at all.
> To push her away, with no glimmer of hope—and no trace,
> My cycle's complete; I can finally leave this awful place.

In fact, my mother kidnapped me and my sister away from my father. She took us halfway across the country, and no one would tell him where she went (she took us from Seattle, to Michigan). The following Christmas, in despair he walked out to the end of a long pier, took off his shoes and set them at the edge of the pier, and jumped into the freezing waters of the Puget Sound. He was only thirty-seven years old. I never really knew my father, but was following his example all my life. Now, I was standing at the end of the pier, with my toes hanging over the edge—so to speak. The question was, to be or not to be.

My friend Arthur had shown me compassion a few days earlier, when he forgave me for not having his money. I really wished—in the same way—I could get my son's forgiveness. But he was only three months old; he wouldn't be able to understand any of this for years. Then suddenly, something like a light turned on in my mind; it was a revelatory insight, an answer to the reason why my father's ghost was suffering so severely. He needed *my* forgiveness! But like my son—he can't communicate the need to me, because he's on the other side"!

Then just like before, his tormented spirit was again kneeling in front of me, crying. Evidently, he had no idea about what was about to happen. Again I stood up and raised my arms towards the sky, but this time my palms were open and facing heaven, like little radar dishes. With my arms raised up to the sky, I cried out, "Father!—I forgive you"!

In what seemed like a billionth of a billionth of a second, he was gone—freed from a purgatory of anguish. Right away, above where his ghost just was—to be precise, directly over the area where his right shoulder was a second before—a bright light, like a piece of burning magnesium appeared. And within it, was the growing emanation of a group of "higher evolved spirits", that is to say, angels looking down on me. Evidently, they were gathered there because this type of thing didn't happen very often, and they were there to witness it, or something. Instantly, I went from not believing in angels, to thinking they've been floating around me the whole time, watching me do every bad thing I'd ever done. I buried my face in my hands and felt the kind of guilt and shame you feel as a child just before receiving a beating.

Abruptly, all the dread and shame melted away, and I was overcome with feelings of love and compassion. Thankfully, spiritually evolved beings don't judge afflicted people like me harshly—they only have love and compassion for us. It's that we judge ourselves harshly.

In their company, I went through a kind of life review, acknowledging every bad thing I'd ever done, or that had been done to me, and I forgave everything. I wanted to make amends to everyone that I'd harmed, but there was no way I could possibly track down all those people. I didn't know the names of most of the people I ripped off, or otherwise hurt. The only option was to repent, and forgive myself.

So, in the presence of the higher-evolved spirits, I proceeded to acknowledge every shameful thing I'd ever done and that was done to me, and I resigned never to do any of those things again. Afterwards, in a kind of trance the last part of the poem came "through" me:

Through self-observation, with clarity I see,
These are negative cycles I must break to be free.
Awoken and out of the hole,
I forgive my father, freeing his soul,
Feeling our redemption and forgiveness for all.

Break the negative cycles,
Be free of bad programming,
And create your destiny.
Be patient and kind; don't tell lies,
Live, give and apologize.
Have faith in yourself, and forgive,
And for heaven's sake, learn what love is.

It was nearly four in the morning, when I finished the poem. Weird gooey tears had been gushing from my eyes, and streaming down the side of my face all night, dripping off my chin like a leaky faucet. The tears all landed in the same spot, on the left knee of my jeans, creating a wet-spot about four inches around. And my lips were starting to chap from dehydration.

From beginning to end, the vision lasted about nine hours. Afterward, I was tired and dehydrated from crying all night. So I went into the kitchen to get something to drink. Upon entering the kitchen, I noticed a small plant sitting on the table. It hadn't been watered since before Madeline left. Right away, I put myself in the place of the dying plant and felt its desperate thirst for water, and life.

I grabbed a glass and filled it with water. I tended first to the plant, then drank several cups myself (Jonah 4:10). Then I went to bed. As I was lying in bed, a disturbing thought entered my mind. I feared the feelings of renewal, gratitude and joy— would be gone in the morning. Like some weird acid trip, after a good night's sleep, I'm going to wake up to my typically miserable self. With that thought in mind, I went to sleep.

After a short rest, I awoke with the sunrise on the seventh day of the new millennia. Outside, the storm had subsided. Upon remembering the events of the previous night—I noticed the good feelings were still there! With this realization, I jumped up and screamed, "YYYYYYYEEEEEEESSSSSSS"! I was bursting with joy, saying out loud, "I fixed myself"! Then I quickly thought, "No! God healed me"! I spent the next couple hours shouting "Thank you God"!—"Thank you angels"! "Thank you, thank you, thank you"! I was jumping up and down, shouting out in jubilation, like a child who's just received the greatest birthday present of his or her life. I said aloud, "This must be how it feels to win the lotto"!

After reading the poem I thought, there's no way that last part came from me. I'm a hardcore dude, a crab fisherman, I couldn't write something like that. I figured it must've come from the "divine beings" or from God through them, or something.

I knew my father was no longer suffering in his purgatory—and if he could answer my question, "What do you think about your son now?" I reason his answer would be he loves me, and is well pleased. (Matt. 3:17, Mark 1:11 and Luke 3:22)

The thought also occurred to me—as I was jumping up and down, bursting with joy, and extreme gratitude—someone got the story of the resurrection wrong. Something like *this* must have happened to Jesus and Buddha. It must've been what started them off on their careers. And if it initiated them, why can't the same hold true for me? This is when I realized it was my calling, to become a holy man.

While pondering this, I said aloud "I need someone strong to guide me". And again, a light-bulb flashed in my mind, and the answer came to me. So I exclaimed, "I know", "God can guide me"!

The deficient person I'd become, was like a hardened clay image I didn't like, but was nevertheless stuck with. The vision was like water that softens hard clay, giving me an opportunity to smash the image into a formless lump and create myself anew. No longer would I be a product of my childhood environment.

Later that morning, my friend Erin came over with her baby daughter, Gabrielle. I could barely contain myself as I gave her my first testimony. She was glad in her heart when she saw me so happy. As I was reciting the poem to her, she began to cry. And when I was done she stood up, raised her arms, and forgave her mother. Erin was the first person—besides me—to be affected by the vision.

That afternoon I called my mother and invited her and my step-dad over to explain what happened. When they arrived we sat down, and I gave them my second testimony.

Before, I had trouble remembering phone numbers, but remarkably, now I was able to recite the entire poem without even looking down at the paper. By the time I finished, my mother was in tears. The first thing my step-dad said—before he had a chance to think about it—was, "You got lucky".

When my step-dad was young, just five years old, his father Joseph Hill—after whom he was named—also died tragically. His father was a WWII fighter pilot who was killed by friendly fire during the battle for the Philippines. It seemed like my step-dad never worked through the loss. He went through his whole life, with a big chip on his shoulder.

At any rate, he married my mom when I was the age he was when his mother remarried—another example of a repeating cycle. After my mom quit sobbing, she said, "You're not going to believe this, but a couple of days ago I got down on my knees and prayed—for the first time since I left the Catholic Church—for any angels or deceased loved ones to please help my son"!

Of course, I believed her.

Then again, by the next morning they'd changed their minds completely. They started believing that instead of a spiritual experience, I was suffering from "a progressive mental illness".

Regardless of what people believed, I was walking around in a state of bliss; everything seemed to sparkle like new. I honestly believed myself to be the luckiest man alive. On my friend Arthur's answering machine, I left a message saying, "Arthur, call me when you get home, I found the Holy Grail"! The next morning, I gave Arthur my third testimony while driving to get river rock for the pond project.

When I got to the part of the poem where it says, "Be patient and kind, don't tell lies", he interrupted me by saying "No, lying protects us from emotional and physical harm". And just as the words left his lips, BAM! A rock or something hit the windshield about an inch below the rear-view mirror, causing a softball sized circle of glass to shatter, sending tiny shards towards are faces. Arthur reacted quickly, saying "Maybe not".

[Note: Lacking guidance, in the beginning I mistook my rebirth for full enlightenment. Figuratively speaking, I confused pulling the sword from the stone—for finding the Holy Grail.]

For some reason, I didn't want my "stuff" anymore. I looked at the couches and tables, the TV, stereo, DVD player, espresso machine etc., and didn't want any of it. So I told Madeline she could have everything in the house. I left with just a small backpack a few days later. However, before I left, a demolition crew came in and tore down the dilapidated house across the street, greatly expanding my view of Puget Sound and the Mukilteo ferry crossing. The expanded view was a good metaphor, for my expanded consciousness.

Below is the letter my mother wrote to the chief administrator for Snohomish County Mental Health, forty days after my spiritual experience.

Dear Ms. Wolke,

To begin with I have tried repeatedly via several mental health organizations to get help for my son. The level of frustration is extremely high when dealing with bureaucratic rhetoric. My son Scott has had mental problems from very early on. When he was a youngster and his ability to concentrate seemed very limited, I arranged for him to be seen by a psychiatrist. I recall the doctor didn't seem to have any specific information regarding his behavior. He tested Scott for dyslexia, which Scott did not have and that was the end of that. We have since discovered that Scott had attention deficit disorder. If he were treated early on perhaps things would have taken a different course. At any rate, from the age of ten years it has been a series of problems: drug rehab, counselors, problems with the law, school officials etc., etc., etc. Two years ago at the age of thirty Scott went into a deep depression; he was prescribed the anti-depressant Paxil.

He continued the use of this prescription for about six months. He met a girl and fathered a child. The girl took the child and left him two months ago. Since then, Scott has crossed from being borderline to full-blown manic psychotic.

He is completely detached emotionally. He says he loves all of humanity as much as he loves his child. When asked the following day by a Compass Health representative if he would be all right never seeing his son again, his reply was yes. On February 13, Scott called begging me to come and rescue him from his "desert island", meaning the house he is living in and must leave in a few days. On February 14, he called saying he was "going home". When asked what he meant, he said he was going home where he should have gone a long time ago. I took this to be an overt suicide threat and called CDMHP. They in turn called 9-1-1. The police found him outside some restaurant. He denied that suicide was his intention. The police officer arrested Scott on a warrant and put him in jail. Therefore, he did not get the mental evaluation and help I had so desperately hoped for. The warrant was for domestic abuse—maybe that could have been a clue? Scott was evaluated by the Compass Mental Health representative. It was determined that he was manic psychotic and needed help. She then went outside to her car and called CDMHP. They apparently felt that he was not quite crazy enough. After all, he has yet to kill himself or cause damage to others on a physical level. Just for the record, Scott's father committed suicide, as did his father's uncle. It would seem to me that there is an inherited pre-disposition toward mental illness in his family. My feeling is that if he were treated long ago, maybe he would never have gotten to this place. If he were committed to a hospital, perhaps he would have a chance for a normal life. He will not volunteer for treatment; after all, he is another messiah. Why would he need help? I truly feel that I have exhausted all avenues. I feel there are opportunities for people in the mental health profession to help my son. Because he is apparently not "crazy enough", he will go on until something terrible happens to himself or someone else and I will hold those who have repeatedly disregarded my pleas for help directly responsible for any outcome that should arise from his actions. I would appreciate any assistance you might be able to give me. I hope you and your family are never put in a position of having to experience this kind of pain. It is truly heartbreaking. You are the chief administrator for the care of the people of Snohomish County. I hope you can find some way to help my son. Thank you for taking the time to read this letter.

Sincerely, Donna Hill

My mother and brother-in-law showed up at Erin's. Her son Robert answered the door, turned toward the living room, and yelled, "Scott, your mother and brother are outside!"

I said to the people there, "You're the ones giving me the benefit of the doubt and a place to stay like my parents should be". (Matt. 12:47)

It was a sunny spring morning. As we walked over to get into the car, Erin came over to where we were standing, and she said clearly, "Scott, you always have a place to stay here with us; you're like part of our family. We love you unconditionally"!

She made sure to say it loudly so that my mother and brother-in-law could hear.

As we pulled up to Stevens Hospital, I was feeling hopeful. I was sure the psychotherapist would know about abreaction and ego-collapse, and could help me explain it to my family. But my mother wasn't taking me to a psychotherapist.

After giving the receptionist my information, I went back to the waiting area. Outside, my younger brother, James, was pulling into the parking lot, so I ran outside to greet him. I hadn't seen him in a while. After greeting him with a hug, I gave him a summarized version of my poem and experience.

In response, he smiled and said cheerfully, "I welcome this"! Evidently, he was the only one in my family who thought forgiving my father and repenting my sins was a good thing. James sat in the waiting area, as my mother, brother-in-law, and I, were led into a small, windowless room, empty, except for a small stainless steel table, and a hospital bed.

After a few seconds, a man in regular clothes came in, flanked by two orderlies. Assuming he was the therapist, I moved to shake his hand, but he recoiled. Confused and offended, I bowed respectfully, and introduced myself.

He ignored my introduction and asked, "Do you feel like hurting anyone?"

I said, "No". And then he asked if I felt like hurting myself. I said, "No, absolutely not"!

He wrote something down on his clipboard, and before looking up, he asked if I was homeless. I said, "No, I'm—"

But before I could say anything, my mother cut me off, saying, "Yes, he is! He's homeless"!

I maintained, "That's a lie"! The doctor ushered my mom out of the room—leaving me with my brother-in-law. I asked him, "Why did my mom lie like that?"

He said, "I don't know". A police officer came in, shuffled Bruce out of the room, and then quickly shut the door again. I mumbled under my breath, "They didn't just lock me in here?" I tried to turn the knob, and sure enough it was locked. At this moment in time, all of a sudden I noticed numerous dents and scrapes all over the walls.

On the other side of the door, someone was being reprimanded for leaving the table in the room. As if I were going to pick it up, and use it as a weapon against them. And someone else was saying, "Be careful, men, he's an Alaskan crab fisherman. He's probably stronger than he looks"!

A line from the film, *Elephant Man* came to mind. I stood up, and stepped towards the door. In my best British dialect, I said to those on the other side "I am not an animal—I am a human being"! Then I sat back down on the bed with my hands on my lap. The door burst open, and three policemen rushed in. They looked crazy. I tried to reassure them, calmly saying, "If you think I'm going to fight you guys, then you're all delusional, and you need to talk to that man back there", I said as I pointed to the diagnostician who came in behind.

The police ignored me. Two grabbed my arms, and the third held my legs. Then a female nurse walked in holding an enormous hypodermic needle. It was disturbing, to say the least. I protested, "Don't I at least have the right to know what you're shooting me up with?"

The doctor said grimly, "We just need to give you a tranquilizer", and with the three police holding me down, the nurse shot me up.

After a few seconds, the doctor said, "OK, we're going to have to give you another one", as the nurse pulled out another enormous needle. Then it struck me that they weren't trying to sedate me; they were trying to knock me out.

Confused, I slurred, "You said you were going to give me a shot—singular, not a couple of shots; I guess you're all a bunch of liars". Then I passed out.

The next morning, I woke up in a hospital bed, wearing pajamas for the first time since childhood. It took a few minutes to collect my thoughts. Then I got up and talked to a psychiatrist. After a run of simple questions, he asked, "Do you believe you are Jesus?"

I paused for a moment, and replied, "Well, metaphorically".

At this point half the people thought I was crazy, and the other half thought I was blessed by the Holy Spirit. My friend Erin was experiencing a positive change, but I thought, if I am crazy, I'm leading her into my delusion. So I put the poem aside and started trying to figure out what really happened to me. It took fourteen years of studying alone to do this to my satisfaction, and this is my report.

CHAPTER 3

§

THE RESURRECTION ARCHETYPE

NUMBER SEVEN IS FIRMLY ESTABLISHED in all the epic myths and religions. Examples are the seven days of creation (Bible), the seven chakras (Hindu), the seven heavens (Islam), and seven steps of the Buddha. The Zuni creation myth mentions seven golden-grains— to be held between the thumb and four fingers— that men are to be guided by and in the Mayan creation myth, Seven Macaw is a great talking bird with jewel-encrusted teeth that sits atop the tree of life.

Some believe the religious significance of the number seven originated about sixty-five hundred years ago, with Sumerian astrologers who first noted the seven planets. That is, the five planets visible to the naked eye, Mercury, Venus, Mars, Jupiter, and Saturn—sun and moon. But evidence suggests it was much earlier.

In 1946, French archaeologist A. Leroi Gourhan discovered seven cave bear skulls—ceremoniously arranged around a stone altar—in a cave outside of Grotte des Furtins, France. Four old skulls surrounded three younger ones (resembling the chakra system). The find dates back to the upper Paleolithic, around thirty thousand years ago.

Anthropologists assume our ancestors revered cave bears, like the Lakota tribe—of the Great Plains—worshipped the buffalo. Reverence for the master animal is universal. But there may be something more going on with the cave bear skulls. Consider the basic symbolism involved.

Skulls are a symbol for death worldwide, and the cave bear emerging from their den—after several months of hibernation—is an obvious metaphor for resurrection. Therefore, it stands to reason the significance of the cave bear skull was that it was a twin symbol for both death and resurrection. In the Chauvet caves of Southern France, the skulls were set facing the entrance, the beginning of the mystic's experience. Then the deeper the shaman goes into the cave, represents the deeper they go into the mystic's experience.

Twenty-five thousand years later, the same idea is present in the design of the Tabernacle, a portable temple the Jews used, while in transit, from Egypt to the Holy Land. Instead of a cave bear skull, there's a golden lampstand decorated with almond blossoms set at the entrance. Past that is the table with four legs and four golden rings, then the five scarlet veils, etc.

However, now there are two different types of menorah the temple menorah with seven lamps—a modern symbol for the state of Israel—and the Hanukkah menorah with nine lamps. The Hanukkah tradition and the nine fold lamp came into being after the defeat of Antioch IV, by Judas Maccabeus and his brothers, in ca. 165BCE. It symbolizes "the Miracle of the Cruz of Oil".

"According to tradition, only a one-day supply of non-desecrated olive oil could be found for the rededication, but that small quantity burned miraculously for eight days. Eight days is how long it takes to press and prepare new oil. Jews commemorate this event by lighting candles for the eight nights of Hanukkah. The ninth candle is used to light the other eight"

(FROM MICROSOFT ENCARTA, A DIGITAL MULTIMEDIA ENCYCLOPEDIA PUBLISHED BY MICROSOFT CORPORATION FROM 1993 TO 2009)

The sevenfold lamp was also meant to embody something specific. It was originally designed to symbolize the archetype for visionary initiation. That is to say, it stood for the most multifaceted vision, ego-death, and spiritual rebirth possible, the sevenfold shaman initiation.

When a prophet complains that "the lamp of God has gone out"! The prophet is actually saying that the spiritual authority lost the teaching on visionary initiations and rebirth—that the lamp stands for—and hence has lost the ability to *recognize* a genuine visionary initiation when it occurs. This is what happened to Jesus at the age of thirty. He experienced the ultimate visionary initiation and rebirth, but the Sadducees and Pharisees couldn't discern it. They could tell red sky at night sailor's delight, and red sky in the morning means sailors warning, but they couldn't discern that Jesus had his visionary initiation on the new moon like Jonah. The resurrection of Jesus on the third day is a metaphor for an archetypal visionary initiation and spiritual rebirth he experienced at age thirty.

> "Those who say that the Lord died first
> and then rose up are in error, for he rose
> up first and then died. If one does not first
> attain the resurrection while alive, when
> they die they will receive nothing".

(THE GOSPEL OF PHILIP, NAG HAMMADHI
LIBRARY, 200CE, ORIGINAL TRANSLATION OF
THIS TEXT WAS PREPARED BY MEMBERS OF THE
COPTIC GNOSTIC LIBRARY PROJECT OF THE
INSTITUTE FOR ANTIQUITY AND CHRISTIANITY,
CLAREMONT GRADUATE SCHOOL)

The spiritual authority didn't recognize his visionary initiation and his family thought he was losing his mind (Mark 23). Nonetheless, he knew intuitively it was what happened to the prophets, to get them started. The reason why John says, "You should be baptizing me", and "I'm not worthy to untie your sandals", is that unlike the Sadducees, John *recognized* Jesus's vision and rebirth for what it was.

Nonetheless, the truth about Jesus's spiritual rebirth was lost behind the metaphors that represent it. The fables are meant to convey—using clusters of symbols—a transit, from darkness, to light. But taking religious metaphors literally, blinds you to the true meaning.

The Lampstand

There are seven single lamps that together make one; observably, the more wicks you light, the more light they give off. Likewise, there are seven possible facets to prophetic visionary initiations, which in principle, can be experienced during one archetypal vision. For example, a visitation from a divine being can—through fear and trepidation—inspire a genuine repentance, whereas a visitation from a lost loved one can heal feelings of loss and bereavement. If both folds are experienced during one vision, they gain the therapeutic value of both, and so on.

The lampstand was decorated with almond blossoms. Almond blossoms are another twin symbol for rebirth. Blossoms symbolize rebirth because they only appear after the death-like state of winter dormancy. Also, almond trees are the first-fruit trees to blossom in spring, thus symbolizing the first type or archetype for rebirth.

The Seven Folds of Visionary Initiation

* Crying out in affliction
* Visitation from a divine being
* Visitation from a lost loved one

- ❧ Abreaction of an early traumatic event
- ❧ Formulation of a new religious code
- ❧ Seventh day advent
- ❧ Third dark day to new moon advent

CRYING OUT IN AFFLICTION

It should be common knowledge that it's possible to initiate a life-changing visionary experience just by crying out in affliction when you're exhausted and sleep deprived. Spiritual experiences happen without crying out. But the line of prophets who begin their careers by crying out goes all the way back to the beginning.

> "You shall not afflict any widow or fatherless
> child, if you afflict them in any way, and they
> cry out to me; I will surely hear their cry".

> (EXOD. 22:22)

The burning bush is another "twin" symbol for rebirth. Bushes and foliage go dormant in winter, then they bud and blossom in spring. As well, fire is a symbol of death and resurrection, because it burns down the forest, which fertilizes the soil for new growth.

Really, Moses was the one crying out; the murderer was in *his* burning during a vision, and from the ashes of that spiritual experience, a greenhorn holy man emerged.

> "The children of Israel cried out in affliction
> to God… And God looked upon the children
> of Israel, and he acknowledged them".

> (EXOD. 2:23, 25; MOSES IS SPEAKING
> FIGURATIVELY ABOUT HIMSELF)

"O Lord my God, I cried out to you, and you have healed me. Oh Lord, you have brought my soul up from the grave; you have kept me alive, that I should not go down to the pit".

(Ps. 30:2)

"And the lintels of the doors were moved at the voice of him that cried out".

(Isa. 6:4)

"I called on your name, O Lord, from the lowest pit. You have heard my voice…"

(Lam. 3:55–56)

"I cried out to the lord because of my affliction, and he answered me. From the depths of the grave I called for help, and you listened to my cry…The earth with its bars closed behind me forever; yet you have brought up my life from the pit, O Lord, my God".

(Jon. 2:2–6)

"And when the morning star rose they [subterranean humanity] blinked excessively as they saw its brightness and cried out that surely now the sun-father was coming; but it was only the elder of the Bright Ones, gone before with elder nations and with his shield of flame, heralding from afar the approach

of the Sun-father! And when, low down in
the east the Sun-father himself appeared,
even though he was shrouded in the middle
of the great world waters, they were so
blinded and heated by his light and glory
that they cried out to one another in anguish
and fell down wallowing and covering their
eyes with their bare hands and arms"

(Zuni Creation Story, 5 of 6; brackets mine)

"So Zipacná cried out from the pit where
he was hidden, shouting from the depths.
Then the boys hurled the great log violently,
and it fell quickly with a thud to the bottom
of the pit. Let no one speak! Let us wait
until we hear his dying screams".

(Popol Vuh, chapter 7)

"And about the ninth hour, Jesus cried
out with a loud voice, saying, My God,
My God, why have you forsaken me?"

(Matt. 27)

The pit symbolizes our lower animal nature and afflicted ego consciousness. You can't escape from this dark space without some help. The pit is equal to the lower waters, the root structure of the tree of life, bowels of the boat, and any other subterranean place away from the light. The pit is also identical to the three lower levels of the ark, where the animals stay; the three lower cave worlds, where humanity starts off swathed in darkness and filth (Hopi); and the three lower chakras that represent our lower animal nature (Hindu).

Note, I cried out to my father who had forsaken me, "Hey, Dad what do you think about your son now?" And after forgiving him I wrote, "Awoken and out of the *hole*".

Visitation from a Divine Being

Fear and trepidation can inspire genuine repentance. Numerous holy men and women have experienced this interaction with a divine being at some point, also called a theophany or hierophany. Listed below—in chronological order—are examples from around the world.

> Then he said, "I am the God of your father, the God of Abraham, the God of Isaac, and the God of Jacob". At this, Moses hid his face, because he was afraid to look at God.
>
> (Exod. 3:6)

> "And the child Samuel ministered unto the Lord before Eli. And the word of the Lord was precious in those days; there was no open vision. And it came to pass at that time, when Eli was laid down in his place, and his eyes began to wax dim, that he could not see; And before the lamp of God went out in the temple of the Lord, where the ark of God was, Samuel was laid down to sleep; That the Lord called Samuel: and he answered, "Here am I".
>
> (1 Sam. 3:1–11)

"Then the Lord spoke in a vision to the holy one and said, 'I have laid help upon one that is mighty; I have exalted one chosen out of the people. I have found David my servant; with my holy oil I have anointed him".

(Ps. 89:19, 27)

"Now it came to pass in the thirtieth year, in the fourth month, on the fifth day of the month, as I was among the captives by the River Chebar, that the heavens were opened, and I saw a vision of God".

(Ezek. 1:1)

"I looked up and there before me was a man dressed in linen, with a belt of the finest gold around his waist. His body was like chrysolite, his face like lightning, his eyes like flaming torches, his arms and legs like the gleam of burnished bronze, and his voice like the sound of a multitude. I, Daniel, was the only one who saw the vision".

(Dan. 10: 1–7)

"In the second watch of his enlightenment, When the mind was thus concentrated, purified, bright, unblemished, rid of defilement, pliant, malleable, steady, and attained to imperturbability, I directed it to the knowledge of the passing away

and reappearance of beings. I saw—by
means of the divine eye, purified and
surpassing the human—beings passing
away and reappearing, and I discerned how
they are inferior and superior, beautiful
and ugly, fortunate and unfortunate
in accordance with their karma".

(BUDDHA, PALI CANON)

"As he neared Damascus on his journey,
suddenly a light from heaven flashed around
him. He fell to the ground and heard a voice say
to him, "Saul, Saul, why do you persecute me?",
"Who are you, Lord?" Saul asked. The Lord
said, "I am Jesus, whom you are persecuting".
He replied. "Now get up and go into the city,
and you will be told what you must do". The
men traveling with Saul stood there speechless;
they heard the sound but did not see anyone".

(ACTS 9:1–9)

"When he [Muhammad] was about forty years
old, an Angel holding a scroll is said to have
appeared to him in a vision, and commanded
him to "write"! "Recite thou, in the name
of thy Lord; who created man from clots of
blood: Recite thou! For thy Lord is the most
beneficent, who hath taught the use of the pen;
hath taught man that which he knoweth not"".

(KORAN, SURA XCVI; BRACKETS MINE)

Unfortunately, few female examples exist. Saint Joan of Arc had a famous vision, in a field in France, in the year 1424. She saw figures identified as Saint Michael, Saint Catherine, and Saint Margaret, who inspired her to overthrow the English and bring the Dauphin to Rheims for his coronation.

"On the evening of the twenty-first of September [1823], While I was thus in the act of calling upon God, I discovered a light appearing in my room, which continued to increase until the room was lighter than at noonday, when immediately a personage appeared at my bedside, standing in the air, for his feet did not touch the floor".

(Joseph Smith, Book of Mormon)

"And the oldest of the Grandfathers spoke with a kind voice and said: Come right in and do not fear. And as he spoke, all the horses of the four quarters neighed to cheer me. So I went in and stood before the six, and they looked older than men can ever be—old like the hills, like stars. The oldest spoke again: Your Grandfathers all over the world are having a council, and they have called you here to teach you. His voice was very kind, but I shook all over with fear now, for I knew that these were not old men, but the powers of the world. And the first was the power of the West".

(Black Elk Speaks, 21; "The great vision")

A "breakthrough to the sacred" in the form of a visit from God or mythical ancestor happens in the same manner all over the world, though in a variety of different contexts, depending on what the person was taught to believe. For instance, the Buddhist will receive a visitation from the Buddha, or some other Bodhisattva or Buddhist saint. A Christian will behold a vision of Jesus, angels, the Madonna, or some Catholic saint. A Hindu will see Krishna or some other Hindu god or saint, etc. Divinities don't cross cultures except by word of mouth.

VISITATION FROM A LOST LOVED ONE
There are countless examples of this to be found in literature ranging from the Bible and Shakespeare to Harry Potter. Accordingly, there are thousands of psychiatric case studies of people seeing, feeling, or otherwise interacting with a departed loved one. Having a dream or vision of a loved one at the time of his or her death is a prime example of visionary phenomena. Mary Madeline's vision of Jesus in the garden after his crucifixion is an example of this. She just lost someone dear to her. He said, "Don't cling to me". Jesus taught her about nonattachment.

"It's commonly reported that the deceased person has communicated in some way, either by giving a sign or causing things to happen with no rational explanation. It's equally common for people to wake in the middle of the night, lying in bed, or even to walk into a room and think they see their husband or child".

(JUDITH SKRETNY, VICE PRESIDENT OF THE LIFE TRANSITIONS CENTER QUOTED FROM VOELL, 2001)

ABREACTION OF AN EARLY TRAUMATIC EVENT

Abreaction—a psychoanalytical term—more often than not involves spontaneously accessing or "recalling" a traumatic event previously repressed, or "safely" hidden away in one's memory. It involves re-experiencing a traumatic event, in order to purge the "memory" as well as the emotional toll or trauma associated with it.

To fully re-experience something the individual has repressed, or attempted to forget is often a "cathartic" event that can produce release and a "lightness of being" much like opening a valve on a pressurized vessel. Reactions vary with every individual. Some will explode with violence, others will experience profound sadness, yet others are "happy" for the first time in perhaps years, and they will laugh uncontrollably in response. The experience is unique to each person, as we're unique, and the subject's reaction may appear inexplicable to an observer. Precisely because we *are* each unique, judging such an experience for "merit", authenticity etc., is not useful.

"Analysts are delighted by abreaction, live (in the therapeutic sense) for it, and firmly believe that it provides the fastest and most profound relief from all manners of psychological symptoms. Others may be less certain of this, viewing this sudden emotional state with alarm, and frantically searching for ways to calm down what their administrations have disturbed. All therapists should have a clear idea of what is actually happening and should understand a very important fact—handled properly, abreaction can do only good for your client. I have worked with the abreactive state for a good many years now, seeing thirty clients a week for most of that time, and I can promise you that there is nothing to fear from it, as dramatic and traumatic as it can appear to be. It cannot cause your client harm, and it cannot leave the person worse off than before he or she came to you, no matter what you might read to the contrary, as long as the process is completed.

"So what exactly is it, and how do we handle it?
It's the revivification of a traumatic experience
that occurred in a moment of great trauma.
This can be so realistic, as far as the client is
concerned, that his or her body will actually
reproduce the physical changes that occurred
at the time of the event. It can be difficult
for the caring individual to sit and watch
this event, which is so evidently full of pain,
unfolding in front of him or her, but once you
have experienced the sense of lightness and
relief that a client can manifest immediately
after the abreaction has subsided, you will
have no more problem with that. There is
something of immense importance when
working with abreactive states, and that is
to make ABSOLUTELY CERTAIN that
your client accessed the emotional 'roots'
of the psychological difficulty. It is the
ORIGINATING CAUSE OF TRAUMA
(often called the initial sensitizing event or
ISE) that we are after and nothing else will do.
Mostly, abreaction of the sort discussed in this
article appears as the result of regression-style
therapies, but it can also happen spontaneously.
Even then, the rules are the same: work through
it and make sure you've got it all out".

(ABREACTION: THE PSYCHOLOGICAL
PHENOMENA HYPNOTHERAPISTS EITHER LOVE
OR HATE, HTTP//:WWW.HYPNOSENSE.COM/
ABREACTION.HTM, 1996, TERRENCE WATTS)

Abreactions yield a remarkable sense of lightness and relief. Then again, if you can't remember the trauma, because it happened too early on, how can you abreact it? In fact, PMR visions can seamlessly parallel a long-forgotten trauma—thus allowing the necessary emotions to be felt in order to abreact it. The false memories that plague regression therapists are a hallmark of this type of visionary experience.

FORMULATION OF A NEW CODE
The code of Wovoka is a simple example.

> "Be good and love one another and
> don't fight or steal or lie".

(WOVOKA, 1989)

About twenty-five hundred years ago, during the "fourth watch" of his enlightenment, the Buddha formulated "the four noble truths and the eightfold path".

(1) That life is full of suffering,
(2) That suffering is caused by desire,
(3) That the cessation of desire leads to the cessation of suffering,
(4) The cessation of desire can be found by following the eightfold path.

The eightfold path is to attain:

(1) The right views	(5)—The right livelihood
(2) The right thoughts	(6)—The right effort

(3) The right speech   (7)—The right mindfulness
(4) The right action   (8)—The right concentration

The Ten Commandments clearly added to Moses's spiritual charisma. It would have been the prime example here if it had happened during his PMR vision. But according to the story, the Commandments were given to him three months after his vision, evidently by elders who were wise enough to know his visionary initiation lacked a code.

(1) I AM the Lord Your God; you shall have no other gods before me
(2) Do not make graven images
(3) Do not take God's name in vain
(4) Keep holy the Lord's Day
(5) Honor your mother and father
(6) Do not kill
(7) Do not commit adultery
(8) Do not steal
(9) Do not lie
(10) Honor your neighbor's goods

The people have forgotten, but I'm here to remind everyone. If you don't follow the teacher's precepts, you're not following them at all. These are some of Jesus's:

Love your enemies
Forgive and you will be forgiven
Do unto others as you would have done to you
Bless those who curse you
Pray for those who spitefully use you and persecute you

Do good to those who hate you
As I have loved you, you also must love one another. (John 13:3)

According to historical record, Mohammed's vision occurred in a mountain cave outside Mecca, Saudi Arabia in the year 610 CE. As the story goes, an apparition appeared before him and commanded him to recite in God's name, so he began to write the Quran. In it, he wrote (among other things), that there is only one God, the creator of heaven and earth. He expounded on the distribution of wealth—that the rich should treat the poor justly—and be honest in their business dealings.

SEVENTH DAY ADVENT

This fold happens when the vision begins on the evening of the sixth day of the solar cycle (January 6), and lasts until early in the morning, so that after a short rest, the forthcoming prophet wakes up with the sunrise, spiritually resurrected on the seventh day.

> "Hence in all fables and myths the gods appear in a seventh epoch, period, or cycle, as in the Genesis account of the finishing of creation on the sixth day. A series of old allegories placed the rising of the Savior out of death on the seventh morn, and this construction the Christians followed in the institution of Passion Week. With the coming of the seventh or spiritual intelligence, and the bringing of peace. The same Egyptian word, "hetep," which means seven, also means peace and is the name of the Egyptian messiah, Iu-em-hetep, he who comes as the

seventh, and he who as the seventh brings peace
to the seven elementary forces of blind nature.

(ALVIN BOYD KUHN, THE BEACON, 1934)

The Feast of the Epiphany is in fact the earliest known Christian holiday, predating even Easter and Christmas. However, the word epiphany does not appear in the New Testament. The earliest reference to Epiphany as a Christian feast was in the year 361CE, by Ammianus Marcellinus. He said that January 6, is *hemera genethlion toutestin epiphanion* (Christ's "Birthday, that is, His Epiphany.) He also asserts that the miracle at Cana occurred on that day. However, it says in the biblical narrative, the miracle of Cana happened on "the third day". This isn't a contradiction; it's a reference to the lunar calendar, and the return of that first sliver of light, the new moon, after the three dark days.

THIRD DAY TO NEW MOON ADVENT
In the same way the sixth and seventh days link the shaman to the sun cycle, a vision on the third dark day and new moon ties them to the lunar cycle. PMRs that happen during a full moon and during an eclipse are of this fold.

> "Then the Pharisees and Sadducees came, and
> testing Him asked that He would show them
> a sign from heaven. He answered and said to
> them, When it is evening you say, it will be fair
> weather, for the sky is red", and in the morning,
> "It will be foul weather today, for the sky is red
> and threatening". Hypocrites! You know how
> to discern the face of the sky, but you cannot
> discern the signs of the times. A wicked and

adulterous generation seeks after a sign, and no
sign shall be given to it except the sign of the
prophet Jonah. And He left them and departed".

(MATT. 16)

The "sign of the times" they can't discern, is Jesus's visionary
initiation happening on the third day as it transitioned to new
moon. By saying, "no sign shall be given to it, except the sign of
Jonah", he means to say, the only miracle you're going to see, is
that my anointing vision happened on the new moon, as it did
with Jonah. Jesus knows being spit out of a whale onto dry land
on the third day, is a reference to Jonah's visionary initiation
and rebirth happening on the third day—new moon.

"As did Osiris in Egypt, on 'the third day' in
the moon. The new moon was born on the
third day of the dark period. And this, be it
known on authority, was the origin of the
three days during which all Saviors in ancient
scriptures reposed in the tomb of death"

(ALVIN BOYD KUHN, THE BEACON, 1934)

Anointing visions were a rare event. For it to happen naturally
on the seventh day of the sun cycle in conjunction with the
return of the light of the new moon after the three dark days,
was most remarkable—hence the legends.

The King James timeline of biblical events (and that of most
scholars) dates the birth of Jesus at 4 BCE and his death at
33 CE (at thirty-seven years old). On the following page, the
NASA moon phase calendar substantiates that it was indeed a
new moon—in Cana of Galilee—on the seventh day of January,
in the year 26 CE, when Jesus was thirty years old.

NASA moon phase calendar for Cana of Galilee, 26 CE, New Moon, January 7

Year	New Moon	First Quarter	Full Moon	Last Quarter	ΔT
26 Jan 7 16:34	Jan 14 21:52	Jan 21 17:11	Jan 29 11:10	
Feb 6 07:24 A	Feb 13 04:53	Feb 20 06:54	Feb 28 07:15	
Mar 7 19:18	Mar 14 11:25	Mar 21 21:30	Mar 30 00:57	
Apr 6 04:28	Apr 12 18:45	Apr 20 12:32	Apr 28 15:31	
May 5 11:43	May 12 03:53	May 20 03:37	May 28 02:45	
Jun 3 18:13	Jun 10 15:26	Jun 18 18:26	Jun 26 11:04	
Jul 3 01:14	Jul 10 05:40	Jul 18 08:44	Jul 25 17:21	
Aug 1 09:52 T	Aug 8 22:30	Aug 16 22:11	Aug 23 22:53	
Aug 30 20:58	Sep 7 17:29	Sep 15 10:35	Sep 22 05:07	
Sep 29 10:55	Oct 7 13:33	Oct 14 22:02	Oct 21 13:24	
Oct 29 03:39	Nov 6 09:00	Nov 13 08:53	Nov 20 00:37	
Nov 27 22:34	Dec 6 02:01	Dec 12 19:37	Dec 19 15:00	

The truth about Jesus's visionary initiation and his true teachings has been lost to history for nearly two thousand years. The feast of the Epiphany—a Catholic holiday celebrated on January 6—is one of the last remaining remnants of that occurrence. This 7x7-fold pattern outlined in this book, is a restoration of the first accord, the true Bride of Christ.

The word prophet means seer. People think that means to see the future. In reality, adepts can see the meaning of arcane religious metaphors most are "blind" to.

WHEN MOSES THE MURDERER WAS IN HIS BURNING

The burning bush passage has mystified people for thousands of years, but most likely, it would've been familiar to the

Egyptians living in his time. The literate would've certainly recognized it as a plagiary of spell 108 of a holy text we now call the Egyptian Book of the Dead.

Moses probably learned to read and write by reciting these Egyptian religious scripture, as Muslim children in that area still do today with the Koran. Below, from the Egyptian Book of the Dead, is the prototype for Moses's burning bush passage. Both are metaphorical references to visionary initiation and rebirth. In this context, the snake represents transformation and renewal, because snakes shed their old skin.

"As for that mountain of Bakku where the sky
rests, it is in the east of the sky. A serpent is
on the top of that mountain. I know the name
of this serpent which is on the mountain; its
name is, He Who is in His Burning. Now after
a while he will turn his face against Re and
a stoppage will occur in the sacred bark and
a great vision will occur, for he will swallow
up seven cubits of the great waters; Seth will
project a lance of iron against him and he will
vomit up all that he has swallowed. Seth will
place him before him and will say to him with
magic power, get back at the sharp knife, which
is in my hand! I stand before you navigating
aright and seeing afar. Cover your face, for I
ferry across; get back because of me, for I AM
the male! Cover your head, cleanse the palm
of your hand; I AM whole and will remain
whole for I AM the great magician, the son of
Nut, and power against you has been granted
to me. Who is that spirit who goes on his

belly, his tail and his spine? See, I have gone
against you, and your tail is in my hand"

(EGYPTIAN BOOK OF THE DEAD,
CAROL ANDREWS, UNIVERSITY OF
TEXAS PRESS, 1991, 113)

The text below is from Exodus, chapter 3, "The Burning Bush
Passage".

"He led the flock to the back of the desert,
and came to Horeb, the mountain of God.
And an angel of the lord appeared to him in a
flame of fire from the midst of the bush. Then
He said, "Do not draw near this place. Take
your sandals off your feet, for the place where
you stand is holy ground." And Moses hid his
face for he was afraid to look upon God".

(EXOD. 3:1, 5–6)

"Then Moses said to God, Indeed, when
I come to the children of Israel and say to
them, "The God of your fathers has sent
me to you", and they say to me, what is
his name? What shall I say to them? And
God said to Moses, "I AM, who I AM".

(EXOD. 3:13)

"So the lord said to him, what is that in your
hand? And he said, A rod. And he said, Cast it on
the ground. So he cast it on the ground, and it
became a serpent; and Moses fled from it. Then

the lord said to Moses, Reach out your hand and
take it by the tail (and he reached out his hand
and caught it, and it became a rod in his hand),
That they may believe that the Lord God of
their Fathers, the God of Abraham, Isaac, and
Jacob has appeared to you. Furthermore, the
lord said to him, now put your hand in your
bosom. And he put his hand in his bosom. And
when he took it out behold, his hand was leprous,
like snow. And he said, put your hand in your
bosom again. So he put his hand in his bosom
again, and drew it out of his bosom and behold
his hand was restored like his other flesh".

(EXOD. 4:2–8)

Spell 108 mentions a purging, during a "great vision" that happens
after turning away from Re; Moses also hid his face from God.
Both passages take place on an eastern mountain. On one there is a
burning bush and on the other, a great snake, named "He Who is
in His Burning". Both stories include the cleansing or regeneration
of hands. Both are given a gift of the gods—a knife versus a staff—
and most importantly, both pick up a snake by the tail. Snakes, fire,
and bushes all symbolize regeneration. Picking up the snake by the
tail—and taking it to the Fathers—is a figurative reference to him
taking his vision to the elders, to give them testimony.

The place Moses was standing is holy ground by virtue of the
vision happening there. Another example of this is Bodh Gaya,
in northeastern India. The place is considered holy ground
because that is where the Buddha received his enlightenment.

Fire is a universal metaphor for the necessary burning away
of a person's animal nature and distended ego to make way for
a rebirth of the self. The Phoenix rising from ashes is perhaps
the best-known example.

"The Phoenix", according to the most developed
forms of the story, is a bird about the size of an
eagle, brilliantly colored in plumage; it is either
purple with a golden collar, or a dazzling mixture
of red, gold, and blue. It is the only one of its
kind and lives in Arabia. At the end of an epoch,
as it feels death drawing near, it builds a pyre of
the sweetest spices, on which it then sits, singing
a song of rare beauty. The rays of the sun ignite
the nest, and this and the bird are consumed
to ashes. From the ashes there arises a worm,
which eventually grows into a new phoenix".

(*Man, Myth and Magic*, BPC
Publishing, 1970, Vol. 16, 2185)

In any case, bringing repressed trauma into the light of day can
be extremely therapeutic. Even so, it usually involves bringing
up some deeply personal issues. It's normal to feel uncomfort-
able talking about it—most would rather keep it private, and
that's fine. However, from time to time these visions are more
of a public matter than a personal one. This is particularly true
when a new code for the people or seeker is formulated (i.e.,
new commandments are given).

CHAPTER 4

§

NEW WINE, FALSE PROPHETS AND TWINS

MOST SCHIZOTYPAL PROPHETS WILL STAY stuck in the delusions of their visionary experience, "set in the east". Precious few have the humility to question their vision and transformation and thus embark on the spiritual quest. As was stated earlier, paradoxically, to progress from this initial stage of spiritual development, one must see a vision as subjective (i.e., see it as an inner experience, a figment of the mind, produced at a time of stress), then set it aside and work to gain knowledge.

In the passage below from the Gnostic gospel of Mary Magdalene (part of the codex found in Nag Hammadhi, Egypt, in the 1950's), Jesus asserts that visions don't come from the soul or spirit; they come from the mind.

> "I said to Him, Lord, how does he who
> sees the vision see it, through the soul or
> through the spirit? The Savior answered
> and said, "He does not see through the soul
> nor through the spirit, but the mind that is
> between the two that is what sees the vision".

(GOSPEL OF MARY MAGDALENE, CHAPTER 5:10–11)

Significant spiritual truths *do* come from PMR visions (e.g., compassion, forgiveness, gratitude, repentance, joy, etc.). But the highest places of spiritual understanding don't come from overnight visions. The way to the "high places" of spiritual understanding is by putting forth spiritual effort, taking instruction from a wise adviser, or seeking knowledge alone for many years. Spiritual rebirth should correspond to the beginning of the mystic's experience, not the middle or end.

After the vision—yet before taking in any tangible knowledge—the greenhorn prophet is symbolized by a set of twins. They start off having been depressed and ready to die from their youth up, host to the spirit of darkness and ignorance. After the vision, suddenly, the heart is opened, and the spirit of regeneration is upon the prophet. At this point, the spirit of ignorance and the spirit of regeneration are both active and working together in the shaman, like a conjoined twin. Whenever you have a twin reference like Seth and Osiris, Flint and Sapling, Sodom and Gomorrah, wicked and adulterous, Sadducees and Pharisees, etc., the scribe is indicating this level of consciousness. The Saul/Saint Paul dichotomy designates his or her status at this level.

Considering the propensity for schizotypal charismatic prophets to split the group and start new dynasties, in all likelihood, the founders of Rome, Remus and Romulus, probably weren't actual twins, but were instead a schizotypal prophet at the level of the twin who changed his name from Remus to Romulus.

THE SEVEN CHAKRAS

The chakra system was originally designed to be a graphic representation of the degrees of human religious consciousness. Like a growth chart or road map, it's a visual aid—depicting different levels of spiritual understanding—not something to believe or disbelieve.

Akin to many other journeys to skillful competence, there's a standard hierarchy from spiritual ignorance to full enlightenment. The ascending and descending lines of the chakra system are a relatively modern way to chart out that progression. Before numbers, sages used the natural landscape, from the lowest conceivable place to the highest (e.g., the bottom of a deep pit, or lower waters to the top of a mountain), and the tree of life, from lowest subterranean root, to the topmost branch.

"What is the matter with you that you deny
the greatness of God, when He has created
you through different stages of existence?
Do you not see how God has created the
seven heavens one above another".

(QURAN 71:13–15; NOAH)

The three lower chakras (consumption, lust, and power), symbolize spiritual darkness, our lower animal nature. Plants and animals have been fighting over these three things forever. The first or "root" chakra is situated at the base of the spine, between the anus and genitalia. Here we start, growing by consuming food, sights, sounds, smells, feelings, knowledge, traumas, etc. Then when we hit puberty, and the sexual organs mature, the second chakra opens, and *lust* becomes part of our experience. The second chakra—called the "sacral"—is located at the level of the sexual organs.

The third chakra is located at the level of the solar plexus. It symbolizes the controlling and dominating *power* of the alpha male animal.

The three lower centers are personified by awful characters like the wicked Graeae sisters of Greek mythology (the three blind witches who must share one eye), and the three-headed dog Cerberus, guardian of the underworld.

The ancient Egyptians believed that after you died, Osiris judged you in front a tribunal of gods during a ceremony called "the weighing of the heart". During the ritual, the dying person's heart was set on a scale and measured against a feather called Maat. If you had a heavy heart—any heavier than a feather—Ammit, "The Devourer", a threefold beast with the head of a crocodile, the front legs and body of a leopard, and the back legs of a hippopotamus, would consume you. Likewise, the western dragon is a three-part amalgamation of a reptile, big cat, and bird of prey.

The three temptations, thirty pieces of silver, three days in the tomb, and thirty missing years, exemplify the lower centers in the Christian tradition. Schizotypal leaders stuck at the third chakra, void of compassion, are the real anti-Christs (wicked). Centered at the fourth, the false prophets and their spawn are the spiritually adulterous.

The archetype for the third chakra ruler—for our time— is Adolf Hitler, appropriately titled, the Führer of the Third Reich. Millions of people have sensed Hitler was the predicted "anti-Christ". The main counterargument *was* that the leader of Russia, Joseph Stalin, killed more people than Hitler in WW II. The truth became known at the end of the Cold War, when previously sealed records were released. It turned out, far fewer people died in the Siberian camps as was previously thought. After crunching numbers, researchers found Hitler killed almost twice as many noncombatants as Stalin, who killed around six million five hundred thousand to Hitler's twelve million or so. The underworld lords of myth symbolize men like these—heartless dictators, void of compassion, because that attribute is above them, at the fourth chakra. For the most part, evil men hold all the positions of political power held around the world at this time.

The lower three "ornamental" blossoms on the lampstand that don't hold anointing oil or give off light, are also a reference to the three lower chakras, and our animal nature.

There *is* a constructive aspect to the three lower centers. Without consumption and lust, none of us would be here. However for the shaman, the lower animal nature must be subdued and held securely underfoot. The following text is an excerpt from *The Power of Myth*. In it, one of the world's foremost authorities on comparative religion and mythology,

Joseph Campbell, teaches journalist Bill Moyers the true meaning of the virgin birth.

Joseph Campbell: "The fourth chakra is at the level of the heart, and this is the opening of compassion. And there you move out of the field of animal action and into a field that is properly human and spiritual. Now in each of these centers there is a symbolic form. At the base of the spine, there is the form of the lingam and yoni, the male and female organs in conjunction. At the heart chakra, there is again the male and female organs in conjunction but in gold. This is the virgin birth; it's the birth of spiritual man out of the animal man. It happens when you are awakened at the level of the heart to compassion and suffering with the other person, that is the beginning of humanity. And the meditations of religion properly are on that level, the heart level."

Bill Moyer: "You say that it's the beginning of humanity, but in these stories, that's the moment a god is born!"

Joseph Campbell: "Yeah and you know who that god is? That god is you! All of these symbols in mythology refer to you! You can get stuck out there, thinking it's all out there, thinking about Jesus and the sentiments about how he suffered and all, but what that suffering represents is what ought to be going on in you! Have you been reborn? Have you died to your animal nature and come to life as a human incarnation?"

Bill Moyer: "Why is it significant that it's of a virgin?"

Joseph Campbell: "It's that the begetter is the spirit; it's a spiritual birth...the virgin conceived of the word, but it came through the ear...now the Buddha wasn't born from his mother's side literally, but symbolically, he was."

Bill Moyer: "But the Christ came the way you and I came."

Joseph Campbell: "Yes but of a virgin, and then according to Roman Catholic tradition, her virginity was restored. So nothing happened physically, you might say. It's not a physical birth; it's symbolic of a spiritual transformation. That's what the virgin birth is about."

THE HORN AND HIS WHORE

At first, the shaman has a vision and rebirth to share, but no real scholarly knowledge of the kind one gets by reading a book, because that attribute (spiritual effort) is above him or her at the fifth chakra. Preaching a vision and putting forth spiritual effort by studying alone are two very different things. The problem with the greenhorn prophet is the greenhorn can facilitate secondary resynthesis just by presenting a disclosure of a new vision (new wine) to someone in a vulnerable state of mind.

> "People who join cults usually do so when they
> have been alienated from their friends and family
> and have fallen into a state of pessimism and
> despair. The bizarre belief system of a new cult
> holds out to them the promise of salvation, and
> if they can make the necessary cognitive leap,
> they may experience an ecstatic transcendence
> of their previously miserable existence".

(STEVENS AND PRICE, 154)

Contrary to popular belief, Paul of Tarsus didn't experience a conversion to the teachings of Jesus during his vision on the road to Damascus. Paul never even met Jesus. Rather, he experienced a primary mazeway resynthesis (PMR) of his own. It happened when he was in the process of chasing down—and stoning to death—the original followers of Jesus.

Saul had just watched over the stoning death of Stephen, one of the early gnostic followers of James. Allowing Stephen's death by stoning is just the type of psychological stressor that can facilitate an ego-death experience. But after his vision, Saul went to Arabia and started preaching it right away. He preached his vision for three years, before finally going to Jerusalem and speaking to the actual apostles. By this time, Paul had formulated his own gospel of Jesus, based on his vision, and he was gaining tons of converts (among the spiritually ignorant), via *secondary* resynthesis. The gospel of grace is by definition a gospel based on rebirth.

> "Immediately after the vision he [Paul]
> preached the Christ in the synagogues".
>
> (Acts 9:20; brackets mine)

In Acts, it states four times that after Jesus died, there was "one accord" among the apostles, Mary the mother, Mary Magdalene, and a multitude of believers. This was the first accord, the teaching Jesus commissioned to Peter and James to teach the Jewish elders. Jesus is called the bridegroom; he's married to an endeavor that produces teachings and eventually a church, aka "the bride" Paul's PMR vision started the first schism in the first accord. He preached his vision, a cunningly devised fable for the spiritually ignorant.

> "But when it pleased God, who separated me
> from my mother's womb, and called me by his
> grace, to reveal his Son in me, that I might
> preach him among the heathen; immediately
> I conferred not with flesh and blood: Neither

went I up to Jerusalem to them which were
apostles before me; but I went into Arabia, and
returned again unto Damascus. Then after three
years I went up to Jerusalem to see Peter".

(GAL. 1:15–18)

In other words, after three years of preaching
his PMR vision all over Arabia, Paul finally
went to Jerusalem to talk to the apostles. He
tried to join them, but they were afraid of
him. They didn't believe Paul was an apostle

(ACTS 9:26).

The word apostle means "one who advocates a viewpoint",
so the apostles didn't believe Paul was advocating Jesus's (and
their) viewpoint. Because he wasn't, Paul preached his own
vision of Jesus. Paul could facilitate secondary conversions, and
no doubt, many individual lives were changed for the better.
What's more, he penned some beautiful passages in his gospel
of grace. To be sure, everything he wrote was from the heart,
not from the Lord, or the Fathers, but from *his* own heart. This
is not a good thing.

"I have heard what the prophets have said
who prophesy lies in my name, saying, I
have dreamed, I have dreamed! How long
will this be in the heart of the prophets who
prophesy lies, indeed they are prophets of
the deceit of their own heart, Behold, I am
against those who prophesy false dreams,

and tell them, and cause my people to err
by their lies and by their recklessness".

(JER. 23:25–26, 32)

"And the word of the Lord came to me saying,
Son of man, prophesy against the prophets
of Israel who prophesy, and say to those who
prophesy out of their own heart", "Hear the
word of the Lord"! Thus says the Lord, Woe
to the foolish prophets, who follow their own
spirit and have seen nothing"! Oh Israel,
your prophets are like foxes in the desert".

(EZEK. 13:1–4)

The trickster fox is associated with false prophets, because it lives both underground and on dry land and is notoriously sly about stealing bird eggs, thereby preventing any possibility of emergence or ascension.

Since Paul experienced a genuine PMR, he could naturally facilitate secondary mazeway resynthesis just by giving an account of his testimony—so signs and wonders abound. But he avoided the Jewish elders because they would've recognized him as a false teacher. If they caught anybody preaching their vision, they'd stone the person. In fact, Saul/Paul never moved beyond the second level of transcendence (the fourth chakra), the level of the twin. Accordingly, he wasn't afraid to speak ill of dignitaries. Below Paul says the apostles added nothing to him.

"But from those who seemed to be
something—whatever they were—it makes
no difference to me; God shows favoritism

> to no man—for those who seemed to be
> something added nothing to me".

(GAL. 2:6)

Then he declares himself at least as great as the most eminent of the apostles, in *signs and wonders* (i.e., the ability to facilitate secondary mazeway resynthesis).

> "For I [Paul] ought to have been commended
> by you; for in nothing was I behind even
> the most eminent apostles…truly the
> signs of an apostle were accomplished
> among you with all perseverance, in
> signs and wonders and great deeds".

(2 COR. 12: 11–12; BRACKETS MINE)

The plain truth of the matter is that Paul of Tarsus *was* the false teacher the Old Testament prophets, Jesus, and Peter, warned everyone about. His vision, left unchecked, led to the first schism and the formation of a second church. From it, a thousand more schisms have branched off (e.g., Joseph Smith and the Mormons). Now all the subdivisions of Christianity are offshoots of Paul's second accord, aka, "The Whore". Indeed, modern Christianity is "the abomination of desolation", the prophet Daniel predicted would be set up after the end of the daily sacrifice (the daily sacrifice ended with the destruction of the temple in Jerusalem 68-70CE.)

Scholars of biblical archeology are quick to distinguish between the teachings of the original apostles, from what they call "Pauline Christianity". Below, in his own words, Paul makes a distinction between his teachings and Peter's.

"When they saw that the gospel for the
uncircumcised had been committed to me, as
the gospel of the circumcised was to Peter".

(GAL. 2:7)

In other words, a gospel for the circumcised (i.e., the already initiated Jewish elders), was to be taught by Peter and James—whereas a different gospel, for spiritually ignorant Gentiles was preached by Paul.

The spiritual quest begins if and when the initiate questions his or her vision, and starts seeking knowledge. Paul never made this transition; in fact, he never even started the spiritual quest. He was a preacher of his own ecstatic vision, and a creator of cunningly devised fables, not a seeker or a teacher of higher spiritual knowledge.

When emphasis shifts away from preaching the vision to the acquisition of religious knowledge—the mystic begins the spiritual quest. Pursuing truth, the initiate raises his or her level of spiritual understanding, up from the fourth to the fifth center, at the level of the throat chakra, half-way up the mountain.

False prophets preach their visions; the fivefold messenger has put them aside. By working on their selves and putting forth spiritual effort, they acquire *knowledge*. The vision and rebirth get them past the three, to the fourth psychological centers. Then by putting their vision aside and taking advice from elders, they are groomed into the fivefold shaman.

Greenhorn prophets count the three lower as one, summing them up as the spirit of darkness. The rebirth moves them up from the three lower, to the fourth chakra. But with the fivefold shaman, the three lower centers are each counted separately—one, two, three, four, and five. With the sevenfold shaman, the three lower centers are again counted together as one and summed up as our lower animal nature. The rebirth moves them up to the fourth, which is only the second fold for the sevenfold shaman. So at the third fold of seven, consciousness is equal to the fivefold shaman.

"The uppermost three centers (the fifth, sixth, and seventh) are of increasingly sublimated spiritual realizations: fifth chakra, Visuddha (region of the larynx), of the element Space (akasa, often translated ether), having sixteen smoky-purple petals, a white triangle within, and resounding to the syllable ham. This is the center of spiritual effort".

(JOSEPH CAMPBELL, MASKS OF ORIENTAL GODS: SYMBOLISM OF KUNDALINI YOGA, BRIGHAM YOUNG UNIVERSITY, 1981)

CHAPTER 5

§

THE QURAN CAME INTO BEING, in the same way as the five books of the Torah. Both come from a sacred marriage between the Shaivite elders—and their ancient, oral tradition with transcendent knowledge—to an anointed prophet who could write.

When Moses received the Ten Commandments, and talked "face- to-face" with the lord, he wasn't talking to himself, seeing things, or hearing voices in his head, and he wasn't in the midst of an extended visionary state. Moses was talking with very wise elders, who were in turn speaking as a mouthpiece for their God, El Shaddai, also known as, Shiva the Destroyer. And the angels who dictated the Quran to Mohammed were in fact, direct descendants of those elders recognized and groomed Moses, after his visionary initiation near the city of Midian two thousand years earlier.

After waiting two thousand years for another anointed prophet who could write to come along, logically, after recognizing his anointing vision, the elders groomed him and gave him a book, just as they did with Moses. That is, they recognized Muhammad's visionary initiation, told him to put the vision aside or be put to the sword. He submitted, and they raised him up to be their messenger prophet, thus making him the last great prophet of the processional cycle.

The Quran tells a hidden story of how the Shaivite elders are actually responsible for the religions of the book. After they groomed Muhammad and gave him the book, they called the Jewish elders to a meeting, and told them they raised up another messenger prophet, and given him a book, in a language their people could understand. But when the Jewish elders learned the Shaivite elders groomed another lawgiver like Moses, and gave him another book, the Jews rejected the new messenger and his book, thus breaking a sacred covenant. Moses said a prophet like him was going to come, and that they were to listen to him, but they didn't.

After emerging from the darkness of the lower waters—they traverse the dry land—and climbed halfway up the mountain of God, to where the rainclouds gather, and fresh water rivers originate from solid rock. This is how the fivefold prophets part the waters.

UPANISHADS

The Chhandogya Upanishads are an ancient Hindu holy text. They're one of the primary Upanishads; together with the Brihadaranyaka, they rank among the oldest Hindu texts, dating to the Vedic Brahmana period ca. 800–900BCE. Like Jesus's Sermon on the Mount—the cornerstone of his ministry—the Upanishads were an oral tradition for some time before they were committed to writing, or "doctrine".

MEDITATION ON THE FIVEFOLD SAMAN AS RAIN

> "One should meditate on the fivefold Saman
> as rain. The syllable Him is the wind that
> blows from the east, the Prastava is the cloud
> that forms, the Udgitha is what rains, and the
> Pratihara is the lightning and the thunder.
> The Nidhana is the cessation. It rains for him
> whenever he desires, and he brings rain for

others even when there is no rain who, knowing this, meditates on the fivefold Saman as rain".

(Holy Chhandogya Upanishads,
part 2, India, 900BCE)

Meditation on the Fivefold Saman as Water

"One should meditate on the fivefold Saman in all the waters. When the clouds gather, that is the syllable Him; when it rains, that the Prastava; the rivers which flow to the east, these are the Udgitha; the rivers which flow to the west, these are the Pratihara; the ocean is Nidhana. He does not die in water and he becomes rich in water who, knowing this, meditates on the fivefold Saman in all the waters".

(Holy Chhandogya Upanishads,
part 2, India, 900BCE)

The fivefold Saman is symbolized by the (upper) waters. They're the rainmaker, because they're supposed to be able to call forth rain from a cloudless sky. At the end of Deuteronomy, the last of his *five* books, Moses refers to his teachings as the rain.

"Give ear, O heavens, and I will speak; And hear, O earth, the words of my mouth. Let my teaching fall like rain and my words descend like dew, as raindrops on the tender herb, And as showers on the grass".

(Deut. 32:1–2)

The core teaching of Islam—called the five pillars—is also known as the monotheist creed: There is no God but Allah, and Muhammad is his prophet, pray every day (most pray five times), to fast during Ramadan, give alms and journey to Mecca at least once. The reason why there are five pillars, and why most Muslims pray five times a day, is because the Fathers who groomed Muhammad and gave him the book, were purposely instituting a fivefold-level proxy teaching for the masses, in times of spiritual drought. The elders bring forth a water bearer to keep people from being led astray by false teachers and keep the masses on track for when Shiva returns. If you're worshipping one God, Creator of heaven and earth, the Lord of Hosts, then at least by proxy you're worshipping Lord Shiva (i.e., God Almighty). In fact, the Kaaba Stone is a Shiva lingam. Muslims march seven times around the Kaaba stone and kiss it, exactly like the Shaivite do at the Shiva temple in Varanasi India. The only difference is the Muslims don't know they're venerating Shiva. In the passage below, Muhammad invokes Allah to make rain.

> Anas bin Malik said, "A person entered the Mosque on a Friday through the gate facing the Daril-Quada and Allah's Apostle was standing delivering the Khutba (sermon). The man stood in front of Allah's Apostle and said, "O Allah's Apostle, livestock are dying and the roads are cut off; please pray to Allah for rain." So Allah's Apostle raised both his hands and said, "O Allah! Bless us with rain. O Allah! Bless us with rain. O Allah! Bless us with rain"! Anas added, "By Allah, there were no clouds in the sky and there was no house or building between us and the mountain of Silas". Then a big cloud like a shield appeared from behind it

(i.e., Silas Mountain) and when it came in the middle of the sky, it spread and then rained. "By Allah"! "We could not see the sun for a week".

(HOLY HADITH VOLUME 2, BOOK 17, NUMBER 127)

Native American shaman Black Elk is a modern example of a fivefold rainmaker shaman. Like Moses and Muhammad he was recognized after his vision and groomed by elders. The passage below is from the book *Black Elk Speaks*.

"On the way up to the summit, Black Elk remarked to his son, Ben: Something should happen to-day. If I have any power left, the thunder beings of the west should hear me when I send a voice, and there should be at least a little thunder and a little rain". Of course, what happened is related to Wasichu readers as being merely a more or less striking coincidence. It was a bright and cloudless day, and after we had reached the summit, the sky was perfectly clear. It was a season of drought, one of the worst in the memory of the old men. The sky remained clear until about the conclusion of the ceremony.

"With tears running, oh Great Spirit, Great Spirit, my Grandfather with running tears I must say now that the tree has never bloomed. A pitiful old man, you see me here, and I have fallen away and have done nothing. Here at the center of the world, where you took me when I was young and taught me; here, old) I stand, and the tree is withered, Grandfather, my Grandfather".

"We who listened now noted that thin clouds had gathered about us. A scant chill rain began to fall and there was low, muttering thunder without lightning. With tears running down his cheeks, the old man raised his voice to a thin high wail, and chanted: "In sorrow I am sending a feeble voice, O Six Powers of the World. Hear me in my sorrow, for I may never call again. O make my people live"! For some minutes the old man stood silent, with face uplifted, weeping in the drizzling rain".

Moses receiving the five books, King David receiving the five loaves of showbread reserved for the high priest, and Jesus feeding five thousand with five loaves of bread. All denote the fivefold shaman-level teaching. The fivefold shaman understands their vision was subjective, and how to recognize and transcend it. They are raised up by elders to a place where they can easily distinguish the difference between a wicked ruler (three lower), false prophet (fourth), and fivefold messenger (fifth). They have been given knowledge of one God. Their assurance is spiritual duality; God and heaven are above, the people below.

RESTORATION OF THE BRIDE

Christians are taught Jesus was the same divine being, from his birth in the manger, until his death on the cross. But in reality the mystic's experience doesn't work that way. It never has and it never will. The missing thirty years is a way of saying that the time he spent wallowing in the three lower chakras is missing from the story. It begins with the baptism and him fasting in the desert for forty days. This denotes a transition from the lower three to the fourth chakra.

> "The Pharisees and Sadducees came to Jesus
> and tested him by asking him to show them a
> sign from heaven. He replied, when evening
> comes, you say, it will be fair weather, for the
> sky is red, and in the morning, it will be stormy,
> for the sky is red and overcast. You know how

to interpret the appearance of the sky, but you cannot interpret the signs of the times. A wicked and adulterous generation looks for a sign, but none will be given it except the sign of Jonah. Jesus then left them and went away. When they went across the lake, the disciples forgot to take bread. Be careful, Jesus said to them. Be on your guard against the yeast of the Pharisees and Sadducees. They discussed this among themselves and said, it is because we didn't bring any bread. Aware of their discussion, Jesus asked, you of little faith, why are you talking among yourselves about having no bread? Do you still not understand? Don't you remember the five loaves for the five thousand, and how many basketfuls you gathered? Or the seven loaves for the four thousand, and how many basketfuls you gathered? How is it you don't understand that I was not talking to you about bread? But be on your guard against the yeast of the Pharisees and Sadducees. Then they understood that he was not telling them to guard against the yeast used in bread, but against the teaching of the Pharisees and Sadducees".

(MATT. 16: 1-12)

The sign of the times that the Pharisees and Sadducees can't discern is that Jesus experienced his visionary initiation on the third day and new moon, as Jonah did. Jesus knows being spit out of the whale onto dry land on the third day is a figurative reference to Jonah's anointing vision happening on the third day—new moon.

In the passage above, Jesus is referencing four different levels of consciousness for the schizotypal leader: wicked (third chakra), adulterous (fourth chakra), fivefold (fifth chakra), and sevenfold (whole and complete). In the end, only a few of Jesus's disciples could discern the difference. The twelve baskets symbolize the twelve disciples; because baskets hold bread like good disciples hold teachings. With the five loaves or fivefold level teaching, they're small baskets; with the seven they're large baskets with more to offer. Jesus says, "I'm not talking about bread". He's talking about different levels of religious consciousness for the prophet, and the different teachings they can produce. The fivefold shaman lives in spiritual duality; he's been groomed by elders, to worship a personal God above. The sevenfold shaman *is* that God.

[The Knights Templar excavated the temple in Jerusalem ca. 1118 CE. They seemed to recover something that made them very wealthy, and—at the same time—threatened the Catholic Church. After their dig, the Templars started praying seven times a day, as opposed to the Muslim's five times. They probably found lost gospels that enabled them to draw a distinction between the wicked, adulterous, five, and sevenfold teachings.]

CHAPTER 6

§

DIVINE NECTAR

"The last two stages of the ascending
lotus series are then of the two ways of
experiencing what is known as God,
either as with form or as without".

(JOSEPH CAMPBELL, THE INNER REACHES OF
OUTER SPACE: METAPHOR AS MYTH AND AS
RELIGION, NEW WORLD LIBRARY, 2002, 39)

THOSE WHO PERSEVERE WILL EVENTUALLY transcend monotheism and the religious duality that comes with it. Beyond monotheism, the first mystic's union is with the universe, a feeling of oneness. In this viewpoint, also called "pantheism", the universe is God. Yet in all the ancient traditions, everything with a name and form comes from the goddess, including all the gods with names and forms, because woman brings forms into existence by giving birth.

As above, so below, as a man thinks, so he is, etc. The sixth chakra holds the "third eye". It's not situated to the right or left, but in the middle, representing non-duality.

Where they still have initiation rituals for young girls, at the time of their first menstruation they're put in a hut and told to meditate on what the change means. They eventually realize they are now equal to the earth goddess in her power to bring forth new life; they are just like the goddess—plant a seed in Mother Earth and it will bring forth new life. Now, likewise, she's capable of bringing forth new life and nurturing it. Initiation makes the daughter equal to her biological mother in status under the goddess.

Planting used to be a ritual wherein Mother Earth would agree—after copious supplication by the shaman—to let us damage her so we could eat. This is a mode of environmental consciousness wherein those who love the earth—and share a kinship with our siblings—the plants and animals—will tread softly upon her. Now scientists warn that carbon emissions have been causing global warming and climate change. At this time, the health of our planet is diminishing daily with strip mining, deforesting, deep-water drilling, fracking, excess carbon emissions, etc.

All women are manifestations of the great goddess, the giver of forms. When the "divine nectar", that is, the wisdom and unity of the goddess's teaching is lost, the earth and women suffer. The male creator god is a proxy made up by elders, who stands like a cross-dresser in place of the true giver of forms, the goddess.

SONNET TO THE GODDESS

"The Wise and Invincible One...
The Valiant One...
The One who is worshipped by the gods...
I pay respect to you.
The Venerable and Virtuous One; you are the shelter of all living beings.
Your beauty is Un-manifested yet Manifested.
You are the Terrible Night/Emptiness, the Great Night/Emptiness, the Ender of Time, and the Constant within change.
Your Face is as luminous as a burning meteor; the light of your body is as bright as fire...
Your three eyes are as vivid as the burning flame.
You are the Nurturer of the past, the Shelter of all spirits. But no one is your shelter.
You are the Protector of all gods... I pay respect to you again.
The Goddess of Gods, your brilliance is comparable to billions of suns...
O the shining light of suns, salvage your devotees.
The Auspicious One, you are known as the Nurturer and the Creator of the Universe. I pay respect to you many times.

From you the Universe is created, sustained, and destroyed. You are the Past, Present, and Future. Everyone knows you are the Greatest. I pay respect to you along with all other gods.
The Origin of Ultimate Knowledge, the Origin of Music, the Immeasurably Powerful, I bow down to you O Goddess, you are present in all levels of Creation.
O Bearer of Weapons, your beautiful form, your eyebrows and thighs steal the mind...
You are the Earth; Death and Diseases are you
Goddess, you are the Mother, the Wisest Victorious One, the Nurturer, the Ultimate Warrior, the Will, the Absence of Will, the Killer, the Piercer, the Transcender, the Deathless and the Speaker of the Ultimate Truth".

THE SEVENTH CHAKRA

The seventh chakra is topmost on the Hindu chart. Understanding the ultimate source of the universe is beyond human comprehension, is also called the "honey doctrine", and the "knowledge of Brahman". This is the idea that ultimately, the source of the Universe is beyond pairs of opposites, and beyond names and forms; that is to say, transcendent (i.e., beyond explanation). But at the same time, it's the very ground of your being. At the deepest level, you are the transcendent.

> "These things I have spoken to you in figurative
> language; but the time is coming when I will
> no longer speak to you in figurative language,
> but I will tell you plainly about the father".
>
> (JOHN 16:2)

Jesus used the father and a bright cloud figuratively, to reference the transcendent source, also called Brahman by the Hindu. Brahman is not a name for a god, and it's not to be confused with Brahma, the Hindu creator god, or Brahmin, a title for people of the highest Hindu cast. It's a word that denotes the principal, that ultimately God is transcendent. The passage below—from the Gospel of Thomas—is a declaration of Jesus reaching these high mystic unions, union with form and formless.

> "It is I who am the Light which is above them all. It is I who am the All. From me did the All come forth, and unto me did the All extend. Split a piece of wood and I am there. Lift up the stone, and you will find me there".

> (THOMAS GOSPEL, NAG HAMMADHI
> CODEX, CA. 200CE, SAYING #77)

Brahman (the transcendent mystery), pervades everything; Jesus is in union with this all-pervading, transcendent source energy, so he too must pervade everything. Hence, split a piece of wood. Accordingly, the King James Cyclopedic index asserts that honey represents God's words.

> "May I not fall from Brahman. Verily, for him the sun neither rises nor sets. He who thus knows this secret of the Vedas, for him, there is perpetual day. Hiran imparted this Doctrine of Honey to Praja, Praja to Manu, and Manu to his progeny. And the father told his eldest son this very knowledge of Brahman. A father may declare to his eldest son or any other worthy disciple, this very knowledge of

Honey. And not to anyone else, even if one
should offer him this sea-girt earth filled with
wealth. This doctrine is certainly greater than
that, Yea, this certainly is better than that".

(CHHANDOGYA UPANISHADS III-XI, 1–6)

It is impossible to kill or be killed in the name of a sanctity that
transcends names and forms. The Judas Gospel was another
Gnostic text lost for centuries. Incidentally, Gnostic means, "of
or relating to knowledge, especially esoteric mystical knowledge". In other words, a gnostic was one who knew. According
to the Judas gospel, Jesus took Judas aside, and asked him to
betray him. Then he taught Judas the secret doctrine of transcendence in addition to an esoteric teaching on the procession
of equinoxes explained in the last chapter.

"[Come] that I may teach you about [secrets]
no person [has] ever seen. For there exists
a great and boundless realm, whose extent
no generation of angels has seen, [in which]
there is [a] great invisible [Spirit], which no
eye of an angel has ever seen, no thought
of the heart has ever comprehended, and
it was never called by any name".

(JUDAS GOSPEL, CA. 160CE, SCENE 3)

The transcendent source is beyond names and forms. The
sages say, "No tongue has soiled it, no word has reached it". In
the Judas Gospel, Jesus is speaking about the transcendent in
the same way as the great sage—and founder of Taoism Lao
Tzu—does in the first stanza of the Tao Te Ching.

"The Tao that can be told is not the eternal
Tao; the name that can be named is not
the eternal name. The nameless is the
beginning of heaven and earth. The named
is the mother of ten thousand things".

(LAO TZU, TAO TE CHING, CHINA,
CA. 600BCE, STANZA I, VERSE 1-2)

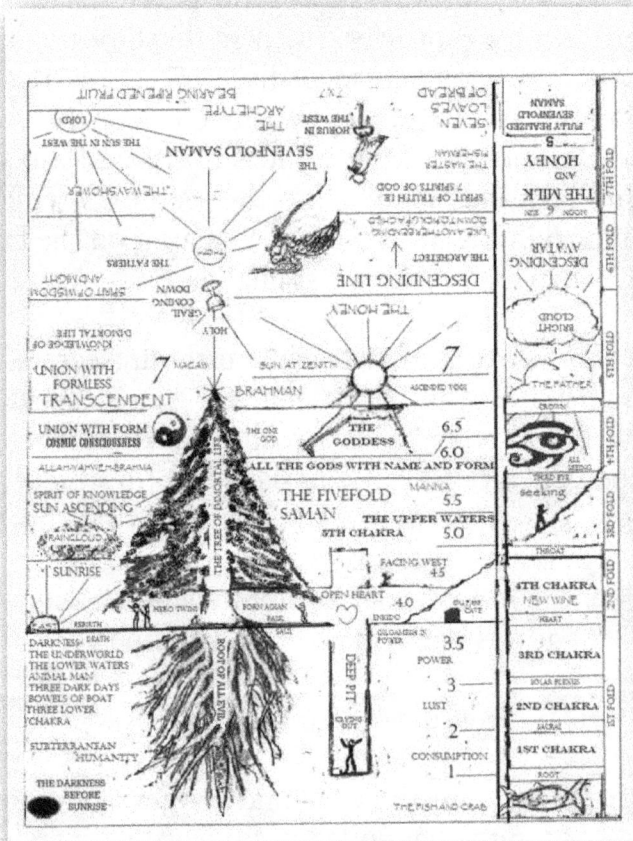

The difference between an ascended master and an angel
of the Lord is that the ascended master—symbolized by an old
wise man with a long, white beard at the top of a mountain— has

attained knowledge of Brahman, and thinks they are fully enlightened, but they're not. They are at one with the father, but have no knowledge concerning the main personifications of Brahman, and the universe (i.e., knowledge of the personal Gods and Goddesses). Truth is the creator God above is a proxy for Shiva, purposely invented by wise elders to keep the masses safe from false teachers, and keep them on track for understanding this end time revelation.

It's true, there's only one transcendent source, but there are many gods. In the end, all men are avatars of the transcendent, all personify the source. Likewise all women are manifestations of the Great Goddess, embodying the Universe. The three main personifications of the transcendent, are called the Holy Trinity. The Bible has the Father, Son and Holy Spirit; that's another way of saying the Creator, Preserver and Destroyer. In the Hindu tradition the Holy Trinity is called the Trimurti. Brahma the Creator, Vishnu the Preserver and Shiva the Destroyer, and they all have wives. Brahma's wife is Saraswati, goddess of knowledge; Vishnu's wife Lakshmi, is the goddess of good fortune; and Shiva's wife, the all-powerful Shakti, is an embodiment of the energy of the universe, and so forth. In the Mayan tradition, the holy trinity responsible for creation is called the Framer, Maker and Heart of Sky. As they were discussing making humans who can speak, one of them says the word "earth". And just by saying the word, it suddenly appears.

The different foods represent different levels of spiritual teachings. Anti-Christs are feeding people bull-shit, false teachers have only wine to share (their vision). Fivefold shaman has the water and the five loaves of showbread (knowledge of one creator God). The goddess teaching is symbolized by divine nectar (non-duality), Knowledge of Brahman is the honey (transcendence), and the seven loaves and milk is the speech and teachings of the sevenfold shaman (i.e., the speech of the Lord shaman). Angels of the Lord know the 7x7-fold pattern, and thus are qualified to groom young prophets into messengers and write scripture.

> "Ho! Everyone who thirsts, come to the waters;
> and you who have no money come, buy and
> eat. Come, buy wine and milk Without money
> and without cost. Why do you spend money
> for what is not bread, and your wages for
> what does not satisfy? Listen carefully to Me,
> and eat what is good, and delight yourself in
> abundance. Incline your ear and come to Me".

(ISAIAH 55:1–3, THE MESSIAH'S
INVITATION TO THE WORLD)

THE VISIONARY ORIGIN OF LANGUAGE

Language is one of humanity's greatest cultural achievements, without which one could argue that Homo sapiens would never have progressed much beyond the Paleo age despite his great brain size. The spoken word is not the only form of complex communication, but it is the principal form of communication among humans, and arguably, it has allowed Homo sapiens to become the dominant life form on earth. Without it, early humans would have found the transmission and retention of knowledge to be extremely difficult, as would complex social behaviors involved in hunting and tribal defense. When and how speech developed is, however, one of the great unanswered mysteries of anthropology.

There are, at present, two main theories of language development: continuity and discontinuity. The remainder of this chapter provides a basis for the discontinuity theory of language development, which at present lacks a mechanism to describe how and why the first person ever spoke. We know, through the study of hearing-impaired and feral children (Eric Lenneberg, Biological Foundations of Language, New York: Wiley, 1967), that there's a period of brain plasticity during childhood, wherein language must be acquired by instruction. So who was the first instructor? And how did that person learn to speak without any instruction?

"Language is a uniquely human trait likely to have been a prerequisite for the development of human culture. The ability to develop articulate speech relies on capabilities, such as fine control of the larynx and mouth, that are absent in chimpanzees and other great apes. FOXP2 is the first gene relevant to the human ability to develop language. A point mutation in FOXP2 co-segregates with a disorder in a family in which half of the members have severe articulation difficulties, accompanied by linguistic and grammatical impairment. This gene is disrupted by translocation in an unrelated individual who has a similar disorder. Thus, two functional copies of FOXP2 seem to be required for acquisition of normal spoken language. We sequenced the complementary DNAs that encode the FOXP2 protein in the chimpanzee, gorilla, orangutan, rhesus macaque, and mouse, and compared them with the human DNA. We also investigated intraspecific variation of the human FOXP2 gene. Here

we show that human FOXP2 contains
changes in amino-acid coding and a pattern
of nucleotide polymorphism, which strongly
suggest that this gene has been the target of
selection during recent human evolution".

(Wolfgang Enard, Molly Przeworski,
Simon E. Fisher, Cecilia S. L. Lai, Victor
Wiebe, Takashi Kitano, Anthony P. Monaco,
and Svante Pääbo, Max Planck Institute
for Evolutionary Anthropology, Leipzig,
Germany, Published online 14 August 2002)

It has been shown that "normal human language" is not possible without the FOXP2 mutation, but there is no reason to
believe that the physical capacity for language would give rise
to speech, other than just vocalizations similar to other animals,
especially in adults who have lost much of the brain plasticity
necessary for rapid language assimilation. So what could have
triggered the development of speech, rather than just vocalization? I suggest that schizotypal individuals subsequent to
experiencing primary mazeway resynthesis (PMR) type visionary states provide a mechanism for the initial development of
language.

A mystery that has baffled scientists for over a hundred
years, is why the gene (or genes) responsible for a disorder
as maladaptive as schizophrenia, continue to exist within the
human genome. The genetic load responsible for the disorder is accountable for low birth rates and early mortality[*], so
why then hasn't the process of natural selection weeded out the

---

[*] (T.J. Crow, Molecular pathology of schizophrenia: more than one disease process?, British Medical Journal publishing group, 1980)

"bad" genes? The answer lies in the fact that most of our genes have multiple functions.

Evolutionary psychiatrists theorize that the genes for schizophrenia are in fact advantageous. They posit that in the same way the genes responsible for sickle cell anemia also confer a resistance to malaria, the same genes responsible for schizophrenia are likewise accountable for schizotypal individuals at what most would call the "better" end of the spectrum:

"Genetic events occurring prior to the migration of H. sapiens out of Africa 150,000—100,000 years ago gave rise to a genetic spectrum that, in its homozygous form, resulted in the schizophrenic phenotype, while heterozygous "schizotypal" individuals possessed cognitive advantages that enhanced their relative fitness. Thus, schizophrenia evolved as a trade-off, firstly, in the emergence of complex social cognition and secondly in the emergence of a phenotype that exhibited unusual creativity and iconoclasm and may be associated with the great cultural and scientific advances of human history".[*]

Said plainly, language was invented by a schizotypal shaman and his son soon after a speech-friendly mutation occurred in a gene called FOXP2 (forkhead box protein P2), about 100,000 to 150,000 years ago. Sometime after the last FOXP2 mutation, a forthcoming shaman—endowed with the new (genetic) advancement—cried out in a pre-speech vocalization of anguish, initiating a "primary mazeway resynthesis" type visionary experience and in doing so, inadvertently reopened plasticity in his brain.

It has been proposed that various religious figures experienced unusual, stress-induced visionary experiences that motivated them to communicate their visions and consequent

---

[*] (Jonathan K. Burns, "An Evolutionary Theory of Schizophrenia: Cortical Connectivity, Metarepresentation, and the Social Brain", *Behavioral Brain Science*, 2004: discussion 855–85, Department of Psychiatry, Nelson Mandela School of Medicine, Durban, 4000, South Africa)

beliefs vociferously. Neuroscientists have recently coined their own term to reference this visionary phenomenon. As the name describes, REM (rapid eye movement) intrusion happens when the REM dream state intrudes into normal waking consciousness. In other words, waking reality is swallowed up by the unconscious. The current explanation for this effect is the assembly and release of DMT (dimethyltryptamine), a powerful hallucinogen synthesized naturally in the human brain during times of extreme stress sleep deprivation.

Unlike someone who has knowingly ingested a mind-altering drug, the person experiencing PMR/REM intrusion has no idea he or she is in an altered state of consciousness. So it is *not* perceived (at least at first) as a dream or vision of any kind. Since it happens during the waking state, the experience seems just as real as any other life experience.

"The condition stems from a bout of "REM Intrusion"—a glitch in the brain's circuitry that, in times of extreme stress, may flip it into a mixed state of awareness where it is both in REM sleep and partially awake at the same time [somnolence]. "The concept that our brain is either 100% awake or 100% in REM sleep is absolutely erroneous. We can have pieces of one state intruding upon another, and that's when things get interesting".*

PMR/REM visions are precisely the type of novel experience needed, in order to excite the nucleus basalis of the brain, which then starts producing brain-derived neurotropic (nerve-growth) factor. BDNF works to speed up electro-chemical transmissions, between synapses**. In short, ecstatic PMR visions can purge emotional traumas etched in the limbic system, and

---

* (Kevin Nelson, University of Kentucky, New Scientist Magazine, Oct. 2006, brackets mine)
** (Norman Doidge, The Brain that Changes Itself, Penguin Publishing Group, London, United Kingdom, 2007, 123)

excite the nucleus basalis to reopen plasticity in the adult brain, thus making the creation and acquisition of language possible.

The assertion is that symbolic consciousness, and by extension language, was first developed by a schizotypal shaman subsequent to the last FOXP2 mutation. After experiencing a PMR-induced resurgence of brain plasticity, a mutant shaman, perhaps shunned for his rapid personality change, and left alone with a small child, simply invented the word as a vocal symbol to name his son and himself then various objects or actions. Due to the active brain plasticity, the shaman and his child could easily remember everything they named. In this way, language could develop separately in different places and spread by diffusion.

If language was a characteristic of the shaman (and his children), ordinary (non-speaking) people would be at a significant disadvantage and the shaman would gain significantly more influence and power within the tribe.

The excerpts below are from the film *What the Bleep Do We Know*, a documentary human consciousness and quantum physics). The scientists are explaining that when Columbus landed in the Caribbean the indigenous people couldn't see the ships. This provides a modern analogue to what was happening a hundred and fifty thousand years ago, as the invention of word and language were being developed.

Candice Pert PhD, "Well, the way our brain is wired up, we only see what we believe is possible. We match patterns that already exist within ourselves through conditioning. So, a wonderful story that I believe is true, is that the Native American Indians of the Caribbean Islands, couldn't see Columbus's ships at all. Because the ships were so unlike anything they'd ever seen before, they couldn't see them".·

---

* (Candice Pert, quoted from the documentary film, *What the Bleep do we Know*, filmed in Portland, Oregon, 2004)

Dr. Joe Dispenza, "When Columbus's armada landed in the Caribbean, none of the natives were able to see the ships, even though they existed on the horizon. The reason that they never saw the ships was because they had no knowledge in their brains, and no experience that clipper ships existed. So eventually the shaman starts to notice that there are ripples out in the ocean, but he sees no ship. He starts to wonder what's causing the effect. So every day he looks, and looks, and after a period of time he's able to see the ships. And once he sees the ships, he tells everybody else the ships exist out there. And because everybody trusted and believed in him, they saw them also".*

A million years ago, in the beginning, the first shaman experience a sevenfold initiation, and is shunned by the group, later culminating in the advent of fire. Eight hundred and fifty thousand years later, the first 7 x 7-fold, fully enlightened shaman and his son invent the word and language. The first words were probably the names God and Son. And one day God pointed up and said to Son, "Heaven". And pointed down and said, "Earth". Before that, no such thing existed in the minds of men, no God was named, and no story told.

One of the thousand names of Shiva is Vagisa, Lord of Speech.

---

* (Dr. Joe Dispenza, *What the Bleep do we Know*, 2004)

CHAPTER 7

§

MASTER OF THE FEAST

"Enough about the fivefold Saman, now for
the sevenfold Saman: One should meditate
on the sevenfold Saman in speech. For him
speech yields milk, which is the milk of speech
itself, and he becomes rich in food and the

eater of food who, knowing this, meditates
on the sevenfold Saman in speech".

(Holy Chhandogya Upanishads,
Part 2, India, 900BCE)

Hindu elders wrote scripture regarding the fivefold and
sevenfold shaman. The five and seven loaves of bread mentioned
in the Bible are figurative references to their dissimilar teachings.
Simply put, the fivefold shaman believes in a personal creator
God, above. The sevenfold has persevered through the mystic's
experience to gain the Knowledge of Brahman, thus becoming a
personification of the transcendent himself (i.e., a personal God).

Fivefold Saman is like the waters, but the sevenfold Saman
is the sun. The elders used the movements of the sun—in seven
stages—to type the experience of the sevenfold shaman, as he
goes from complete darkness to full enlightenment.

"One should meditate on the sevenfold Saman as the yon-
der sun. The sun is the Saman because he is always the same
(sama). He is the Saman because he makes everyone cherish the
same thought: "He faces me", "He faces me"! One should know
that all beings depend upon him (i.e., the sun)".

"What he is before his rising is the syllable Him. The animals depend upon it (i.e., Him). Therefore the animals say Him
before the sunrise, for they partake of the syllable Him of the
Saman (sun).

"What he (the sun) is just after he has risen, that is the
Prastava. Men depend upon it. Therefore men love praise
and eulogy [either direct or indirect], for they partake of the
Prastava of that Saman.

"What he is when the rays go forth, that is the Adi. Birds
depend upon it. Therefore birds hold themselves without

support in the sky and fly about, for they partake of the Adi of that Saman.

"What he is just at midday that is the Udgitha. The Devas (Gods) are dependent upon it. Therefore they are the best of the offspring of Prajapati, for they partake of the Udgitha of that Saman.

"What he is after midday and before afternoon, that is the Pratihara. The fetuses depend upon it. Therefore they are held in the womb after being conceived and do not fall, for they partake of the Pratihara of the Saman.

"What he is after the afternoon and before sunset, that is the Upadrava [approach to the end]. The animals of the forest depend upon it. Therefore they run to the forest and into their caves when they see a man, for they partake of the Upadrava of that Saman.

"What he is just after the sunset, that is
the Nidhana [conclusion]. The Fathers
depend upon it. Therefore they put them
down, for they partake of the Nidhana
of that Saman. Thus a man meditates
on the sevenfold Saman as the sun".

(Chhandogya Upanishads, Part
2, Meditation on the Sevenfold
Saman as the Sun, India, 900BCE)

Seven Steps of Buddha
"When the time for the Buddha's birth grew near, Queen Maya wished to travel from Kapilavatthu, the King's capital, to her childhood home, Devadaha, to give birth. With the

King's blessings, she left Kapilavatthu on a palanquin carried by a thousand courtiers. On the way to Devadaha, the procession passed Lumbini Grove, which was full of blossoming trees. Entranced, the Queen asked her courtiers to stop, and she left the palanquin and entered the grove. As she reached up to touch the blossoms, her son was born, from her right side. Then the Queen and her son were showered with perfumed blossoms, and two streams of sparkling water poured from the sky to bathe them. Then the infant stood, and took seven steps north, and after each step, a lotus bloomed where his foot touched. After the seven steps, he proclaimed, I alone am the World-Honored One"!

Birth stories generally refer figuratively to the holy man's visionary initiation. The Buddha is born from his mother's side (at the level of the heart), like the Hindu god Indra, and the good twin Sapling from the Iroquois creation myth. The evil twin Flint is born first, from the pelvic region, whereas Sapling is born from their mother's armpit (level of the heart). The two streams of water is a reference to the twins.

Immediately after his birth, Buddha stands up, and begins traversing seven steps north. That is to say, after his awakening, he progresses through the seven folds. The lotuses that grow in his footsteps—represent the chakras. North is *up* on a map, so seven steps north signify an ascent up the seven chakra system, from the three lower up to the high places.

"Seven" as a divine-digit or quantity seems apparent nearly everywhere one looks, whether in the physical world, as with the rainbow, musical scale and the Julian calendar, or the spiritual realm, where one finds there are seven possible facets to a prophet's visionary initiation and seven transcendent folds (i.e., seven different levels of religious understanding).

"So I said, I am looking, and there is a lampstand of solid gold with a bowl on top of it, and on the stand seven lamps with seven pipes to the seven lamps. Two olive trees are by it, one at the right of the bowl and the other at its left.

"So I answered and spoke to the angel who talked with me, saying, what are these, my lord? Then the angel who talked with me answered and said to me, do you not know what these are? And I said, No, my lord.

> "What are these two olive trees—at the right of the lampstand and at its left? And I further answered and said to him, what are these two olive branches that drip into the receptacles of the two gold pipes from which the golden oil drains? Then he answered me and said, do you not know what these are? And I said, No, my lord. So he said, these are the two anointed ones, who stand beside the LORD of the whole earth".

(ZECH. 4:5–6, 10–14)

MAITREYA

Buddhist prophecy of Maitreya, aka the "Future Buddha" includes several references to 7 x 7. The arrival of Maitreya refers to a time when the true Buddha Dharma will have been forgotten. The "World Teacher", is found in the canonical literature of all major Buddhist schools

(THERAVĀDA, MAHĀYĀNA, AND VAJRAYĀNA).

"By means of the meritorious power of the
Bodhisattva Maitreya, who will be named Prince
Ajita, three palaces called Vardhamaanaka,
Siddhaarthaka, and Candra, made of the seven
types of gems, will arise out of the earth and
be his residences for the three seasons. Each
palace will consist of seven stories and on each
floor there will be millions of small rooms.
Around each palace there will be seven walls
of the seven types of gems. At the gates of the
palaces will be pandals made of variegated
gems. At the edge of the roofs of those palaces
will be a golden mesh which will make music
similar to that of the five types of instruments.
On top of the palaces seven flags made of
the seven types of gems will be hoisted".

(THE *LOTUS SUTRA*, ORIGINALLY TRANSLATED
FROM SANSKRIT INTO CHINESE BY DHARMARAKṢA,
AKA ZHU FAHU, IN 286CE)

In the King James Bible's Cyclopedic Index, the year of jubilee
held every 7 x 7 years, is a metaphor for Christ's mission.

"Count off seven Sabbaths of years—seven
times seven years—so that the seven Sabbaths
of years amount to a period of forty-nine
years. Then have the trumpet sounded
everywhere on the tenth day of the seventh
month; on the Day of Atonement sound
the trumpet throughout your land".

(LEV. 25:8–9; YEAR OF JUBILEE)

New King James Index Cites:

"Regulations concerning: Introduced by
trumpet every seven times seven years, rules
for fixing prices. The purpose of: Restore
liberty to the slaves, restore the property to
the original owner, remit debt to the indebted
and restore a rest to the land. Figurative
of: Christ's mission, earth's jubilee".

(New King James Version, Cyclopedic
Index, Thomas Nelson Inc., 1983, 187)

The year of jubilee—every 7 x 7 years—is symbolic of Christ's
work.

"The mystery of the seven stars that
you saw in my right hand and of the
seven golden lampstands is this".

(Rev. 1:20)

Seven lamps symbolize the seven visionary folds at the beginning, and the seven stars signify seven transcendent folds (i.e.,
seven stages of spiritual development), ranging from complete
spiritual ignorance, to rebirth, then to putting forth spiritual
effort, persevering to the high places, etc. The 7 x 7-fold mystical experience of Jesus, lead to a teaching and first church.
Peter was commissioned to teach the true bride of Christ, to
the Jewish elders, but the Romans killed most of the people
who knew the first accord, when they leveled the temple and
the city of Jerusalem from 68-70CE. Instead of the truth, the
bride of Christ, we inherited Paul's whore, a cunningly devised

fable for the spiritually ignorant. The 7x7-fold gospel of truth, outlined in this little book, is the true bride of Christ.

Procession of the Avatars

In 2005, the earliest church devoted to Jesus, was discovered in Megiddo, Israel (aka Armageddon), by construction workers doing work within the walls of a maximum-security prison. On the floor of the ancient church, was a remarkable mosaic of two fish, commonly interpreted as relating to the parable of Jesus feeding five thousand people with five loaves and two fish.

The two fish are a reference to the astrological constellation of Pisces. Like the yin and yang, one fish is ascending and swimming to the right; the other is descending to the left. The two fish are symbolic of the union of opposites. They also represent a teaching, about the age of Pisces and an astrological cycle known as the precessions of equinoxes (i.e., the sidereal year, platonic year, great year, processional cycle, etc.), a twenty-five-thousand-plus-year astronomical cycle, and the longest our ancestors could detect with the naked eye. The "end time" prophecies refer to the end and beginning of this cycle, which actually ended and started again on December 21, 2012.

The procession is caused by the gravitational pull of the sun and moon, which causes the earth to wobble slightly on its axis. An effect of this wobble is a very slow movement of the ecliptic (the path our sun appears to trace through the stars), backward through the twelve signs of the zodiac. It's measured by marking the ecliptic, on a map showing the star constellations behind it. Then, seventy-two years later—mark the ecliptic again—and the point will have moved exactly one degree backward, through the 360 degrees of the zodiac. In the Near East, astrologers divided the zodiac into twelve constellations, of roughly thirty degrees (12 x 30 = 360).

In the Near East, an "age" was how long it took for the ecliptic to travel backward through thirty degrees of the zodiac, moving at the rate of one degree, every seventy-two years (72 x 30 = 2160 x 12 = 25,920). Customarily, knowledge of the processional cycle was sanctified, reserved for high priests and kings. The knowledge was typically encrypted into fictions; meant to conceal the truth from the undeserving, and at the same time, reveal it to the worthy.

The Gospel of Judas is a prime example of this. It's no coincidence the scribe used the same numbers in his secret teaching that modern astrologers use to explain the procession of equinoxes.

"Adamas was in the 1st luminous cloud that
no angel has ever seen among all those called
'God.' He [...] that [...] the image [...] and
after the likeness of [this] angel. He made the
incorruptible [generation] of Seth appear [...] the
12 [....]. He made **72** luminaries appear in the
incorruptible generation, in accordance with the
will of the Spirit. The **72** luminaries themselves
made **360** luminaries appear in the incorruptible
generation, in accordance with the will of the
Spirit, that their number should be **5** for each.
The **12** aeons of the **12** luminaries constitute
their father, with **6** heavens for each aeon, so that
there are **7** heavens for the **72** luminaries and
for each [of them **5**] firmaments, [for a total of]
360 [firmaments...]. They were given authority
and a [great] host of angels [without number],
for glory and adoration, [and after that also]
virgin spirits, for glory and [adoration] of all the
aeons and the heavens and their firmament".

(JUDAS GOSPEL, SCENE 4, CA. 160CE)

The numbers 5 and 6 are an encrypted reference to the thirty degrees of an age, 5 x 6 = 30. The teaching is unintelligible, without the help of an adept teacher.

In the Near East, elders divided the processional cycle into twelve, roughly twenty-one hundred year ages. Mayan astrologers split the same cycle into five, fifty-one hundred year ages (5 x 5100 = 25,500). Like other advanced religious systems, the Mayans were expecting the return of Kukulcan at the end of the cycle. The designers of the temple of Kukulcan built it so that on the autumn equinox morning, an image of his mythical form—the feathered serpent—descends from heaven to earth with seven diamonds of light on its back.

The Hindu astrologers equated the processional cycle to a giant day of equinox, rounding it off to twelve thousand years of light and twelve thousand years of darkness. Like the Mayans, Hindu sages expect a Shiva incarnation, at the end and beginning of the cycle, hence his nickname "the Timekeeper". Also one of the thousand names for Shiva is Samvatsarakara, "One Causing the Year".

Near the end of the twelve thousand years of darkness (the Iron Age), the sacred knowledge is forgotten, mankind loses the way, and in a state of mass spiritual ignorance, the people kill the last preserver avatar. Jesus wasn't the first divine being to be killed by an ignorant populace. The Hindu had a word for killing God incarnate long before Jesus was born: Brahmanicide. The fact that there was a word for it long before Jesus, suggests it must've occurred sometime in the past, and someone named it. A society guilty of this sin can gain repentance by selling all their adornments, and giving the money to the poor. Then wearing Rudraksha beads (also called, "the Tears of Shiva").

Two thousand years ago, the religious authority of Jerusalem didn't know what to make of Jesus. The Jews were expecting their warrior messiah—Shiva the Destroyer—to gather up an army and conquer the immoral Romans occupying their land. The plain truth is that Jesus wasn't their God; he was a gentle and approachable preserver avatar, who came to "seek, and save [knowledge] that which was lost".

Currently, all the great religions are expecting "their guy" to show up and convert the rest of the world to their religion. The Hopi are expecting Pahana; the Maya are expecting Kukulcan. While the Jews are still expecting their warrior Messiah, Christians are expecting the second coming of Christ, and the Buddhists are expecting Maitreya. The Shiite Muslims are expecting the twelfth Imam (Mahdi), to come and finish the work Muhammad left undone, and the Hindus are expecting Kalki, the last avatar of Vishnu.

For all those waiting, behold it is I! The Sevenfold Shaman on high! My words will never die! Because the Spirit of Truth is just one, of the seven spirits upon my tongue! I am called, "the First and Last", and my Son is, "the Savior". In the end, indeed the Lamb and Lion manifest together.

> "Look, you have been told everything. Lift up
> your eyes and look at the [bright] cloud and
> the light within it and the stars surrounding
> it. The star that leads the way is your star".

> (JUDAS GOSPEL, SCENE 3; (BRACKETS MINE))